Born to Raise

Pluribus Press, Inc.

Library of Congress Catalog Card Number: 88-061232

International Standard Book Number:
0-944496-02-4

Pluribus Press, Inc.
160 East Illinois Street
Chicago, Illinois 60611

92 91 90 89 88   5 4 3 2 1

Printed in the United States of America

Contents

In every profession, in every act of human enterprise, there are those few who stand alone, as beacons for others to follow. This small group of men and women have visions others cannot conceive, dreams others cannot fathom. Every profession, every field of endeavor, has that remarkable select band of extraordinary achievers. They pierce the heavens. Uncommon temper of will and the courage to dare, they soar as eagles. And just as eagles are born to sweep and spire, in our profession, the great ones, they are born to raise. They are the inspired ones. They rule the world. A rare breed, these inspired achievers. Not yet an endangered species, but in very limited number indeed.

1   Great Expectations

"No young child would ever say: 'I'm going to grow up and become a fundraiser.' If they did, you'd get them psychiatric help."
          —*Richard Berendzen*

When Howard Hughes was asked why, in his later years, he became a long-nailed recluse sealed-up in a dark hotel room, he replied with a shrug and a sense of the inevitable: "I just sort of drifted into it."

"Let me tell you a funny story I heard the other day." That's how my meeting started with Bob Schuller.

I was sitting across the desk from him. Dr. Robert H. Schuller is founder and senior pastor of the Crystal Cathedral in Garden Grove, California. Spiritual leader to a congregation of more than 10,000 members, and a million more through his television ministry, one of the largest in the world. Best selling author.

Schuller leaned far back in his chair. His shirt sleeves rolled up, his collar open, his tie pulled loose. I could not remember seeing him before when he wasn't wearing his clerical robe.

He told his story. "It seems that Oral Roberts, Billy Graham, and Robert Schuller all died on exactly the same day, at precisely the same moment. Each death was totally unexpected.

"St. Peter met them at the Pearly Gate and said: 'I'm awfully sorry, I had no idea that you guys were coming—and here you all are, all at the same time. I have no rooms for you. I can't get you into heaven until we get rooms fixed up. But don't worry, I'll call the Devil and ask him to put you up for a short while until I can get everything ready for you!'

"So St. Peter calls the Devil and says: 'Satan, I've got three friends of mine that need to be taken care of and it won't be for long. I didn't expect them and I just don't have any room for them.' So they all go down below.

"After a very short time St. Peter gets a call from the Devil. 'Pete, you've got to take these guys back. They're driving me crazy. Oral Roberts is healing all of the sick. Billy Graham is having prayer meetings all over the place, saving souls. And Bob Schuller—Schuller is raising money to air condition the place.'"

Schuller leaned far back in his chair and roared.

The story tells a great deal about how Schuller feels about his fundraising prowess, and the role it plays in his ministry. He understands the importance of fundraising. He practices it. He studies it. As we talked, I discovered he has an unmitigated zeal for it!

Few would contest the fact that Schuller is one of the great fundraisers among church people in the world. To build his Crystal Cathedral, he raised in excess of $30 million. In addition to that, he raises a similar amount each year for the annual support of his ministry.

I look around his office. It provides few clues to the man—other than that of a very well organized person. He has many awards, recognitions, and honorary doctorates—but they are nowhere in evidence. The large desk has on top of it only a Bible, well worn. No other papers. I have been told that he is outrageously well organized and operates within a time schedule as tight as a highly strung piano wire.

He told me the story of the building of the Crystal Cathedral. That voice. Unmistakably Schuller.

In 1955, he accepted a call from the Reformed Church in America to go to Garden Grove, California, to start a new church. There was no church, no building, no congregation. With his wife as organist, and with a total of $500 between them, they started off, driving from Michigan with all their worldly possessions packed in an old car.

He searched around and the only thing that seemed to be available for a church service was the old Orange Drive-In Theater. It wasn't being used on Sundays and besides, the parking was good. He paid $10 a week rental. His sermons were delivered from the top of the counter of the snack bar.

As a matter of fact, the Drive-In had parking for 1700 cars. He started preaching four weeks after he discovered the location. He eventually spent six years preaching under the open sky. Soon, the parking lot was full every Sunday.

It didn't take long. The word spread. They came from all over Orange County. They came from all over the country. They drove into the parking lot and attached the speaker to their car window. The growth of his congregation was extraordinary, and led to the first "walk-in/drive-in" church in the country. The church continued to develop and flourish. Finally, the decision was made to build a sanctuary.

"We called in an architect and asked him to design a new church for us. When he brought in his plans, our board was underwhelmed. The problem was, the design was simply drab and ho-hum." Schuller says that taught him one of the first lessons about fundraising. "In order to raise money, you have to have a bold vision. It has to be dramatic and exciting."

He decided to go to a new architect, world renowned Phillip Johnson. I said to him: "Mr. Johnson, I really don't want a building. I want to worship in a garden. God's idea of a church was the Garden of Eden. We have this glorious outdoors all around us—I want to bring it into my church. I want to take the church outside. That's it—I want to take the inside out, and bring the outside in. I can almost visualize it, Mr. Johnson. I want a lot of glass. Yes, yes—that's it. I want a glass structure. I can see it. I want a glass cathedral."

Johnson protested. He told Schuller that even if it could be built—which was questionable—the cost would be prohibitive. "A building like that would be terribly expensive to build, Dr. Schuller."

Schuller then told me that he never asked Johnson what it would cost. He leaned across his desk. There was a pause. A smile. I knew I was about to hear a Schuller postulate. "The reason I didn't ask him what the cost would be was that for years

I had been preaching and living by the concept that no one has a money problem—only an idea problem." He paused, then said to me: "I like that. Put that down! There are no money problems—only idea problems. If you have the right idea, you can raise whatever money is required."

Schuller then returned to the story of the Crystal Cathedral. He told me he said to the architect: "Mr. Johnson, we can't afford a million dollar building, we can't afford a two or three million dollar building, we can't afford a four million dollar building. We can't afford anything! Therefore, it doesn't make any difference what it costs. But I'll tell you this, if you come up with the right idea, we can raise whatever it costs, no matter what the amount.

"Well, after some time, Johnson returned to our board meeting with his design. It was spectacular. It was dazzling. It was inspiring. It was one of the most exciting concepts I had ever seen. We didn't have to have a great deal of discussion. The trustees and I understood at once—the cathedral had to be built. The cathedral had to be built immediately."

Schuller has been described as the major hot-gospeller of fundraising. This is not said in a pejorative way. His appeals have a certain splendor and dignity. What makes him great? What attributes, talents, and skills come together to make him one of the titan fundraisers in the world?

He is a man of limitless energy. That is one of the indicators to his success. I find this same quality in all of the great fund-raisers I know—this boundless energy. In the case of Schuller, he is up at 5:30 each morning, and almost always starts the day with a two mile run. He is an enthusiastic jogger, but then he's enthusiastic about virtually everything he does. Here's another clue: the high degree of zest for work and living. All great fundraisers seem to have that.

He is away from his desk four or five days each week, but almost never misses a Sunday at the Crystal Cathedral. He has learned to work in an airplane. The amount he accomplishes is prodigious. Awesome! He is pastor and spiritual shepherd to both the Garden Grove and the television congregations. He is author of over 20 hard cover books, four of which have made the best seller list. He speaks three or four times a week, every week. He loves it. But there it is again, another guideline. The great fundraisers, they're all hard workers. There appears to be no easy route, no way of avoiding the long hours. But the inspired fundraisers, to them it's not work—it's fun. Schuller's ability to concentrate on a given subject is legend. He is able to block everything else out of his mind until a single problem has been solved or he receives the gift that he has been after. There it is again, still another clue: A single mindedness, a total focus on getting the gift. And with his extraordinary vitality, he can work hour after hour without interruption.

The personal power and presence of the man is of awesome proportions. It is small wonder that major donors from all over the world are attracted to him and to his ministry. He is intense and charismatic. One of his larger donors told me recently: "He simply swept me off my feet." Schuller has been called one of the world's greatest salesmen. He is extremely creative and is described by those who know him as having a magnetic personality.

Schuller feels that his greatest attribute is his ability to listen carefully and respond creatively. Another guideline to successful fundraising: the ability to listen. Perhaps no other skill is as important in our profession.

Schuller told me several stories about how good listening had helped him secure major gifts. But he says that he has another talent which he counts as being even more important to him. "My greatest strength is a God-given gift, and because it is a gift I treasure it all the more. I have uncanny intuition. I can read a situation immediately. And I am almost always right. A psychiatrist who knows me quite well told me one time that I am the most intuitive person he has ever known."

That comment, that passing remark, raised a question of major consequence for me. The important talent of listening, can that be studied and learned? What about intuition? Schuller called it a gift. Can that be learned or are you born with it? And

6**6/   BORN TO RAISE**

of the talents and skills that are really important in fundraising, can they be learned or are you born with them?

Schuller is an impatient man. "Patience is not a virtue if you sit back and wait for your problem to solve itself. There's a time and place for patience and a time to get up and act. You won't start winning without beginning." He repeated that several times during our session. For all of us in this business, that certainly is worth memorizing: You can't win unless you begin.

Impatience may not be considered by all to be an attribute, but I find it in virtually all of the inspired fundraisers I know. Schuller says that he has to move quickly. He says that you see something that has to be done, and you do it. You don't always have the time to wait for a meeting of a committee and then try to get consensus among the group. You have to forge ahead, grab the opportunity.

He has tremendous respect for fundraising and fundraisers. "I find that when we haven't been able to raise money for a specific program, it's not the fundraiser's fault. It invariably means that the project was not right, the dream was not right. Ultimately, the results don't depend on the fundraiser. The project must have integrity, excellence, and urgency." He stopped. Reflected. "I like that. Put that down. That's important—the project must have integrity, excellence, and urgency."

And then I discovered yet another gauge. I find it among all of the inspired fundraisers. Dogged determination. Unrelenting. Unwavering. Schuller has this. They all do.

"Nothing is impossible," says Schuller. "First, the program must provoke excitement and passion. Then explore and exploit the possibility, and subliminate the negative. I will hold onto an idea, if it's really a great one, because I know that it will become possible somehow, some way, with someone's help."

Most of the great fundraisers are inclined by their nature to great expectations. They believe in them, anticipate them, invite them. Somehow, expecting the very most has a way of generating qualities which result in achieving the objective. Counting on success and nothing less, gets into the subconscious, slushes around, and charts the pattern for attainment. Miracles can happen if we put our minds to it. According to Dr. Marcus Bach, a psychiatrist, we all have it within our power to make magnificent and monumental things happen. "Think great, visualize greatness, hope greatly, and be grateful."

The inspired fundraiser won't allow a problem or a lack of money to determine his dreams or his goals. He feels strongly that there is always a way to raise needed funds. He knows that money flows to exciting ideas, visions that have sparkle and dazzle. Good ideas beget good ideas. Dreams inspire creativity and money raising. If the project has magic, funds can be raised.

No minister, priest, or rabbi speaks to more people in the world or in the United States than Schuller. And he would be on anyone's list of top five fundraisers in the world. Is there any mystery why he is one of the great ones? Can the criteria be quantified and qualified? What attributes, personality characteristics, skills and talents go into making an inspired fundraiser?

J. Richard Wilson is president of the National Society of Fundraising Executives. He estimates that there are nearly 20,000 fundraisers in the United States. Add to that all the others who are not full time, not included in his estimate. William Balthauser, the publisher, believes that there may be two or three times that number—perhaps as many as 75,000 men and women who are actively involved in fundraising for their institutions. And he feels that his estimate may even be soft because so many "hide." A college president, for instance, would not be listed as a fundraiser even though he may spend most of his time in that activity. Robert Schuller would not be listed as a fundraiser, although he is one of the best.

Everyday, these men and women shinny up that slippery, greasy fundraising pole. Some reach the top. They don't do it with a smile, the right power tie, a shoe shine, or a strong handshake. And I doubt, also, that it's a case of following Woody Allen's advice: "In order to be successful, all you've got to do is show up 80 percent of the time."

One thing is certain, fundraisers are a totally dissimilar group. They look different. Act differently. Work differently. They are diverse—hard charging and hard driving, quietly effective. They include used-car salesmen types, ministers and priests, scholars and backslappers. Computer freaks and computer-frightened. Great writers and virtually illiterate. They do not have the same characteristics or personalities. The question is: do the really great ones share any qualities and skills? Fundraisers are not, as the former chancellor of the University of California university system, Clark Kerr, described: ". . . as a lightbulb which performs one unambiguous task . . . turned on by someone else at the flick of a switch." The great fundraiser turns on without help and chooses which of many flicks he or she will respond to and how. Lightbulbs are produced by the millions. All have the same components. The fundraiser is a product of background, training, heredity, a mysterious combination of skills, and almost certainly a great deal of luck. But in what combination is this all put together?

Among the finest, most effective in the field, there is at work a magnificent alchemy of mind, spirit, and creative genius that somehow generates sums significantly greater than its parts. What Vincent van Gogh called "the mysterious combinations of kindred tones and vibrations."

What is the secret? Over the long competitive years, what ultimately separates the very finest fundraisers from the merely gifted? In this book, I shall define what makes an inspired fundraiser. The differences are often slight and at times imperceptible. Often, it is a case of those who have "it," win. And those who don't, don't!

What qualities and characteristics are common to the great fundraisers? I have the answer, but I caution you, although the verities and concepts that form the heart and fiber of this book may seem simple, they are deceptively simple. I forewarn you, also, that you may not agree with every thesis I propose. But I am convinced of every plank of my platform.

****

2   Grow or Go

"Some books are to be tasted, others to be swallowed, and some few to be chewed and digested."

—Francis Bacon

"It is because you did not like my first book that you have forced me to write a second one."

—Vladimer Nabokov

There's a reason for this book. A good reason.

You know what just about all of us in this field want. We want our institutions to be the greatest in the country. And we want to be as productive and as effective in our work as we possibly can.

We want to be the best.

To my surprise, when I began my research on this subject, I could not find a single book that dealt in depth with the question of what makes a great fundraiser. What rare combination of attributes and skills make up the inspired ones in this field? There's not a book—not even a chapter. Go ahead, try to find even a paragraph. Nothing exists. How is one to improve if nothing is written on the subject? You begin feeling like Snoopy the Dog: "Yesterday I was a dog. Today I am a dog. Tomorrow I'll probably still be a dog." No chance for improvement there!

The question persisted and gnawed. If identifying these factors is of major consequence and significance to those of us in the field, why is so little written about the subject?

To get my arms around the question and begin the identification, I sent out thousands of questionnaires to professionals in the field of fundraising. I received thousands of responses. You bet the response was high—everyone wants to help in determining the answer to this important question. More about these responses later in the book. But I went one step further.

For me this made the great difference. I interviewed over 50 men and women I consider to be the great fundraisers in the country. Others may be as good, but I honestly doubt any are better. Most of my group would make anyone's list of the top, inspired fundraisers.

I am convinced now that it is possible to quantify the major factors that go into greatness and once that is done, to list these characteristics in some sort of priority of importance. If you want to be the best you can be, this book will lead the way. A wit once described a barometer as an extraordinarily ingenious instrument that was cleverly conceived to tell you the kind of weather you are now experiencing. No barometer, this book! It will list and describe.

I studied these great ones. I spent a day with most of them. Several, I have known for years. We talked, and we argued. But mostly I listened.

These inspired fundraisers helped me design a paradigm of qualities and attributes. But be careful. These great ones are different. The parameters are unruly. No set patterns. Nothing rigid or frozen. My great ones appear to be tall and short, heavy and thin, physically attractive and not so, dressed for success and—well, some not exactly a model of sartorial splendor. No cookie-cutter pattern to follow. Diversity is what best describes the group. I mentioned this to a friend, a member of a prestigious southern institution, who then wrote this ditty for me:

> "So praise them all—big and small;
> And let them have their say.
> Fundraisers never really die, you know—
> They just smell that way!"

Although their lives and careers vary, a common congruity seems to join those profiled in this book. It is their unrestrained and unreserved single-mindedness to be the best. It is much as Winston Churchill said: "I am easily satisfied with the very best." But the book is not about those men and women who are interviewed and quoted. This book is about the lessons they can teach us. The focus is on their characteristics, skills, and talents.

No single factor sets the men and women interviewed apart. It is more a case of doing a dozen things just a little better than average. They tend to be independent sorts and attribute their success to a variety of talents. They often used words as "determined," "creative," and "aggressive" in self-descriptions. They push themselves without mercy, and almost always take work home with them and on vacations. They don't consider themselves workaholics—but by any definition, they are.

William James claims that few of us live up to our full capacity. "Most people live, whether physically, intellectually or morally, in a very restricted circle of their own potential. They make use of a very small portion of their possible consciousness, of their soul's resources in general, and of their potential . . . usually only enough to move one little finger." But there are those within our profession who provide great vitality and inspiration, those who make it a consequential and enlightened calling. I have included many among this group in this book. These are the great ones and their comments and beliefs provide important benchmarks. They dare to go against convention, think big, believe that all is possible, persevere, and create spontaneously and vigorously. This is the story of the celebration of the best in fundraising.

Richard Berendzen is president of the American University in Washington, D.C. He has extraordinary antennae which quiver at even the faintest hint of a large gift. To do what is needed and accomplished at the university, he has had to become its pedagogical leader, its cheerleader, tour guide, architectural visionary, and engaging emissary to the well-to-do. All this in the unending pursuit of resources for the university. He never stops and it never ends. Through his wondrous effort and unrelenting chase for the gift, he rescued this university from near-extinction.

Just like Berendzen, my great fundraisers never stop. No matter what they attain, no matter how big the victory, they never stop. They never stop working. They never stop growing. They seek. They inquire. They probe. They push continuously.

"You've got to grow or go," says Boone Powell, Sr. Grow or go. He is 75 years old, and he has never stopped growing. He is the genius and inspiration that built the Baylor University Medical Center in Dallas. They never used any tax money—local, state, or federal—to build that huge facility. Boone Powell pretty much raised it all himself. Oh, certainly he's had help, but over the years, he has done it pretty much on his own. Hundreds of millions of dollars. Most fundraisers in Dallas concede that he's probably the most effective and inspiring in the city. And those who give those big Texas dollars agree. One major donor to Baylor told me: "I have a lot of places I could give my money, but when Boone asks me, I know it's for something important. I just can't refuse." But Boone isn't alone.

The great ones know that they haven't arrived. Their work is only beginning. And the great ones invest daily in growth enhancement and development training. They hone and polish all the edges of every aspect of their work and performance. I call this "leveraging your skills"—the never-ending process of improving what you've got. Never quite satisfied. Never finished. Never stopping. These great ones, they take their life's cue from Thoreau who said: "Renew yourself completely each day. Do it again, and again, and forever again. To renew is to be alive."

Someone once asked Louis Armstrong: What is jazz? "If you gotta ask what is it," answered Armstrong, "you ain't never gonna know." That's part of the answer. It's an intuitive feeling for fundraising. The great fundraisers know all of the principles, basics, and the mechanics. They know their trade and apply it well. But most of all, they follow their intuition. This is a common thread among all of them. They operate by "gut feeling." No yardsticks, no hoary fundraising rules do they follow. They are led by their intuition. And their intuition is almost always right. Remember the comment by Schuller—he considered intuition his greatest gift. And again the persistent question: Is this a characteristic you can learn, or are you born with faultless intuition. And if you can learn it, why aren't we teaching it?

Also, the great fundraisers are optimists. Cockeyed, pie-in-the-sky optimists. They have a fair measure of their own skill and an intuitive feeling about their prospect. The hunter and the hunted. They are convinced of ultimate success. The great fundraisers are consistent, program after program, year after year. They are not one-shot explosions. They perform regularly, tenaciously, and on target. And they win.

Father Hesburgh is a superb example of what I have just described. The Reverend Theodore M. Hesburgh was until 1987 president of the University of Notre Dame. He is one of the most highly recognized and respected names in America. A recent magazine poll ranked him as the most influential person in education and the third most influential in religion. Most would rank him as one of the nation's greatest fundraisers.

During our session, we were interrupted several times by phone calls. Two I remember were particularly significant. One was from a Cardinal in Rome and the other from the Secretary of State.

We sat in his office, surrounded by books and memorabilia. He was wearing a gray sweater, not necessarily old, but it had surely seen many days of wear in that presidential office. He is a man of many interests, particularly in the fields of theology, civil rights, and aviation. With all his accomplishments and achievements, Father Hesburgh tends to be self deprecating and modest. He is unlike the British prime minister Clement Atlee of whom Churchill once said: "Clement Atlee is a modest man . . . and he has much to be modest about." Father Hesburgh does not have much to be modest about. He has left an indelible mark on his university, on all of higher education, and on this nation. A saintly man. Extraordinary intelligence. Hardly a glimmer of ego. And as tough as they come.

On the Notre Dame campus, I soon heard about what others called "Hesburgh Time." Father Hesburgh is an unrelenting worker, but his schedule is unusual. He rises late, and gets to the office just before lunch time. He usually eats with one of the officers of the university or a priest, goes to the office, makes phone calls and works until evening. After a quick dinner, he returns to the office and works and dictates until two or three in the morning. It is a non-stop schedule.

Father Hesburgh has the longest tenure of any active head of a major American institution of higher learning. He has 106 honorary degrees—that's a Guinness Book world record—and enough awards and citations to fill a large banquet hall, floor to ceiling. Think of all of the chicken dinners the poor man has had to consume in the name of charity and higher education.

He is revered. Father Hesburgh has been a confidant of every U.S. president in recent years. His walls are filled with photographs of scenes from the Oval Office—and photographs of him with recent Popes. He is surrounded by books, shelves of books, a desk piled with books, and a waiting room filled with books. He is obviously a voracious reader. Virtually all of the great fundraisers I interviewed are avid readers. As busy as they are, they steal bits and pieces of time to do their reading. Mostly professional reading, some of an ancillary nature, and as much time as they can grab for leisure reading. But they read.

Father Hesburgh has served on a number of presidential commissions and panels, has been chairman of the Rockefeller Foundation, and is a member of the Chase Manhattan Bank Board of Directors. The list could go on and on.

Of greatest interest, he guided and molded the university for nearly 35 years and during that time, it raised over $300 million in gifts, and secured an additional $306 million in endowment—placing Notre Dame among the top twenty in private universities. The art collection, which consisted of a few paintings along the wall of the old library, is now reputed to be the fifth best collection among American universities, numbering more than 14,000 pieces. During his tenure, the annual budget at Notre Dame increased from $9.7 million to $170 million. A significant part of that budget comes from gifts. Father Hesburgh's advice to me was: "Know your project, know your prospect inside-out, and show enthusiasm. Your presentation must have drive, power, and sparkle." Enthusiasm was a word that kept coming up in interview after interview. Nothing really significant is accomplished without enthusiasm.

He attributes much of his success to just plain, naked luck. I'm reminded of a saying that if you work hard enough, you become lucky. But there's more to it than that. Almost all I talked with told me about their amazing "luck," at virtually stumbling on a prospect at just the right time, under perfect circumstances—as if some unknown higher source had guided them. They call it good fortune, sheer luck. But was it mere luck that put them in the right place at the right time? There can be no question about it. I am convinced that luck is the fortunate result of preparation and opportunity.

Father Hesburgh says: "I'll have to admit I've been very lucky. I think that anyone who's successful, really successful, has an aura of luck about him. There's nothing like being in the right place at the right time—when no one else is there! It's as though you're standing outside and it starts raining dollars from a mail sack that fell out of a plane."

Father Hesburgh told me a story about one of the largest gifts he had ever received. It was announced just the day before my meeting with him. He had been asked by an alumnus to address a luncheon in San Diego. Father Hesburgh doesn't shy away from speaking engagements, but this one was impossible. He had to be on campus the night before and he had an East Coast engagement the next afternoon. He had to decline. But the next day, the graduate called again and persisted. And, he called again. Reluctantly, Hesburgh accepted.

"It meant that I had to fly all night to get to San Diego," Father Hesburgh told me. "I barely had time to shave and shower. I was really upset with myself that I taken on the assignment to begin with. I don't feel I did a good job at all and when I finally came back to the campus, I was really unhappy with myself. A few days later, my secretary came into the office and told me that I had a phone call and said: 'I think this is one you had better take, Father. It's Mrs. Joan Kroc.' Joan Kroc is the widow of Ray Kroc, founder of McDonald's and chair of the Kroc Foundation. She asked if she could come to see me in South Bend.

"We had a delightful meeting. I was very much impressed with her. She had heard me speak in San Diego. She told me that she was greatly taken with my vision for the university and my interest in world affairs. She told me that she wanted to make a gift to the university to establish a program to undergird our work in current affairs. The gift was for $6 million."

He was indeed lucky. He was at the right place at the right time. A school of thought claims that some people are just plain lucky and others are doomed with poor luck and ill fortune. For the luckless, a black cloud seems to follow them around wherever they go and whatever they do. Someone asked Napoleon what he seeks in a general. Without hesitation, he replied: "I look for a general who is lucky." But working hard and working smart must surely be secret weapons. I have never met a lazy lucky fundraiser.

Some fundraisers seem so eager for poor fortune, they race to meet it! Hector Berlioz said that the luck of having talent is not enough—one must also have a talent for luck. The great fundraisers never complain that the cards are poorly shuffled. They almost always are dealt a good hand, or by "luck" draw the right cards.

Many of those I interviewed abhor details. They tend to have much greater relish for thrashing around in the big picture. They are conceptualizers. They are visionaries. Father Hesburgh would certainly be characterized as a visionary, a dreamer, a man capable of seeing the big picture. But he does give weight to the importance of details. "It is my observation that the really great fundraisers actually do extremely well at both the overview and the detail of their work. The best who I know are a combination of innovative planner and imaginative doer, inexplicably linked, one dependent upon the other." There is an old architectural axiom that God is in the details.

However, in this business we must hone our ability to perceive, really work at it. It is this magnified capacity that forges a direct link to reality. Thomas R. Horton says: "They perceive sharply the purpose of their organization and share their perception with others. While their visions for the future are sometimes called dreams, they are neither dreams nor fantasies. Instead, they are clearly etched images of future possibilities, each possibly deeply rooted in the realities of today."

The proper path is quite clear. Always see the big picture, dream the bold dreams—but pay precious attention, inordinate attention to the details. To be successful, you have to do a thousand things better. It's the attention to details that makes the difference. The little things are monumental.

And courage. Father Hesburgh says that courage is one of the important ingredients of a great fundraiser. "I see that quality, personal courage—often lonely courage because everyone else below has passed the buck. If fundraisers do not have the courage to stand alone, quite often, sometimes daily during times of crisis, then they can be in agony. Without courage, it is always a failure. Of that I am sure."

And here we have it, some of those rare qualities. Hard work, luck, courage—and reading, that intellectual thirst.

One additional point occurs throughout. Almost all of the really great fundraisers have been at their institution over a long period of time. They don't jump back and forth, from one job to another. The fundraiser's average tenure with an organization is 11 months. Because of the complexity in identifying the actual number of fundraisers, this figure on tenure will not hold up to statistical substantiation. But it is safe to say that a person cannot be effective on a short-term view. It's not a slam-dunk job.

****

3 Soft Iron into Lead

"Every campaign is a battle. Each campaign you get under your belt means you are ready for the next one. You realize that a lot of blood may flow—including a lot of your own—but that you just live to fight another day. Going through fire is what makes soft iron into lead."

—Theodore Roosevelt

Father Hesburgh spoke to me about courage. The willingness to dare. The exhilaration of taking a chance.

The great fundraisers are entrepreneurial. They have a willingness and an eagerness to break new paths, chart a new course. Their approach is often based not only on vision, but on their innate sense of nascent and challenging opportunity to seek new horizons. It calls for a great sensitivity for potential prospects and patrons, the development of a plan for cultivation, and a willingness to move promptly and effectively where the beacon shines the brightest.

In fundraising, there are the three R's—risk, responsibility, and reward.

"One way to get the greatest satisfaction out of this work and to be the most successful is to look on everything we do as adventure." That's James Lewis Bowers speaking. Jim is the highly successful president of the foundation at Scripps Memorial Hospitals in La Jolla, California. He goes on: "Too many in our business think only of security instead of opportunity. They spend more time worrying about failure than about thinking creatively about success."

All of us in this business need to rattle the traditions of old ways. The tried and true does not always work. There needs to be a roaring disdain for status quo. Following what others have done is too easy, often uninteresting and more times than not unproductive. We find out about ourselves only when we take risks, when we challenge and question. For the really great fundraisers, there is nothing to follow, but everything to discover.

Father Hesburgh says: "I've never been afraid of being different. I don't try to be, just for the sake of being different, but I've always been willing to take a stand and live by it. Sometimes, it is not too popular but I understand, also, that in my position this sometimes happens."

It seems the great leaders, all of the inspired men and women in fundraising, tend to be a little different. And they don't mind it. Many seek the exhilaration, the daring-do of taking the risk. They understand with Samuel Johnson that if all possible objections must first be overcome, nothing will ever be accomplished. Robert Schuller says: "People who worry about answering every possible question and responding to every problem never go anywhere. Take a chance! Take charge! Take control!" The best fundraisers understand that if you want to taste the best fruit of the tree, you have to go out on a limb to get it.

Nationally, within the Jewish community, Brian Lurie is regarded as being one of its keenest and most effective fundraisers. He is president of the Jewish Federation in San Francisco. He says: "I'm willing to take a risk. We've been the best in fundraising because we've been willing to try anything. I'll try anything if it seems right. I believe one of my great strengths is that I'm an innovator." Lee Iacocca says the same: "When times get tough, there's no choice except to take a deep breath, carry on and do the best you can." And then with typical Iacocca inelegance: "Sometimes you have to take an intuitive lead—get off your ass and go."

For a fundraiser, it is simply not good enough to reach what you can. You must reach for what you cannot. I don't know of a better rule. If you want to be all you can be, you have to expect a failure from time to time but you will finally achieve your greatest objective by only standing on tiptoes. In one of his earliest works, Meditations on Don Quixote, Ortega wrote: "A hero is someone in continual opposition to the status quo."

Take the chance. Dare. Grab the opportunity. Nothing great is ever accomplished by a cautious fundraiser. There must be a healthy disregard for the impossible.

An associate of Jim Bowers has called him a fence climber. He keeps climbing over fences, the next higher than the one he has just scaled. Jumping over hurdles he never thought possible. Always seeking, pushing, driving. He confines himself to no fundraising orthodoxy, but charts his own course.

In church fundraising, Ashley Hale is without parallel. My guess is that he has raised more money for churches all over the world than any living person in this business. He says that the mortal enemy of a successful fundraiser is not over-goaling, but fear of failure. But why fear failure? He points out that even in the high jump, you get three tries. And if you never knock the bar off, how will you know how high you can jump. Or if you don't lose a single game all season, he wonders if you might be playing in the wrong league. If you win every time, are you reaching high enough? To succeed magnificently, you must have the courage to fail.

Keep trying. That's the lesson. Bob Schuller told me that if you can conceive it, you can achieve it. "I like that," he said. "Put that down—if you can conceive it, you can achieve it. That's what fundraising is all about. That's how you make dreams come true."

Unless you try something beyond what you have already mastered, you will never grow. A.E. Hotchner says: "Of course we all have our limits, but how can you possibly find your boundaries unless you explore as far and as wide as you possibly can? I would rather fail in an attempt at something new and unchartered than safely succeed in a repeat at something I have done before." You will achieve your very best by reaching for the stars, and following Abraham Lincoln's advice to exercise skilled intelligence to scent out the truth, and the courage to follow this faint light wherever it may lead. I worry about the fundraiser who stops dead in his tracks for concern that any action he takes which is different or out of the ordinary might be wrong. Or if it is right, he is establishing a dangerous precedent. Under these conditions, nothing will ever be attempted for the first time! This is a famous Panas postulate for keeping a fundraiser out of trouble. And out of a job, too!

Courage. Courage to take the risk. There was the Henry IV taunt to the Duke Crillon after a victory at Arques that the Duke missed because "he couldn't find the battle." The king sent him the provocative message: "Go hang yourself, brave Crillon. We have fought at Arques, and you were not there." Courage is nothing more than facing the problems and challenges before us. That's really what fundraising is all about.

Thornton Wilder wrote that every good thing in the world stands on the razor-edge of danger. For the fundraiser, there is always risk. That's inherent in the job. Right or wrong, success or failure, we should be careful to get out of an experience only the wisdom that is relevant—and stop there. Otherwise, we shall be like the cat that sits down on a hot stove lid. She'll never sit down on a hot stove lid again, and that is very well indeed. But, also, she will never sit down on a cold one either.

A corollary to having the courage to dare is combining that quality with a drive for high expectations. The juice has to be worth the squeeze! The successful fundraiser spends his whole life biting off more than he can chew, and then chewing it.

George Engdahl is vice president of the Chicago Symphony Orchestra, one of the world's elite symphonies. And George, one of the elite fundraisers, is in a class by himself. He combines fundraising experience in higher education, health care, and the cultural fields. A great strategist and savvy in all aspects of the profession, he is at his very best at one-on-one contacts. Of him, it can be said that he has the legendary ability to enter a revolving door behind you and come out in front! In our discussion, he told me: "I expect to win. I reach as high as I possibly can. Even higher. I set high standards and then I'm never happy unless I meet my objective. I keep asking myself: 'Hey, how much money have you raised?' I think too often that is why things don't happen. We don't ask that question. We rationalize. I never lose sight of my objective. I have extremely high expectations. And I meet them."

G.T. Smith is president of Chapman College in Orange, California. I don't believe anyone knows what the G.T. stands for. The world knows him as Buck Smith. "Buck" is a very appropriate name for him. But I've never known him to settle for a buck. He's one of the best in the business. He says: "I'm goal-oriented. I have thought a lot about this and have wondered what has encouraged and motivated our board to their highest level possible and I believe that it is that we present them with high expectations. And these high expectations start with the staff."

Buck Smith continues: "You either have high expectations or you don't strive. You don't drive. I feel it is one of the most important qualities in fundraising. It can't be learned. I think that you either have it or you don't."

"I am often asked," says Father Hesburgh, "how an institution solicits support. The answer is quite simple. People support an endeavor that is different and true to what it proclaims itself to be. If we say that we want to be a great university and then compromise our commitment with low standards and permit low performance, we did not deserve to be supported and we will not be. I have high expectations for myself. I haven't fulfilled all of my personal goals. Not nearly. I keep working at it all the time. I push myself all of the time. I feel that there is so much more that I need to do. I always aim high. Very high. If you don't, I don't see how you could achieve very much. I set high goals and objectives for myself and I expect others around me to do the same. And then I count on achieving those objectives."

A great lesson for all of us in fundraising is found in The Book of Job. After thinking about all of the horrible things which had fallen on him like an avalanche, he said: "The thing that I have feared has come upon me." There is a philosophy of work and life, practiced by some: Never expect too much, and you will never be disappointed. If you follow that adage, you will never be disappointed. But do understand, you will never achieve great things either. The successful fundraiser is the one who is disappointed by almost all that he does. Nothing is good enough. The gift isn't large enough, the presentation wasn't dramatic enough. But he will go on, persevere, work even harder to meet his high expectations.

High expectations have to do with both passion and pride. We can take a lesson from Stanley Marcus, former chairman of Neiman-Marcus. He says that he was brought up by a father who was difficult to satisfy because he always felt something could be made or done better. His expectations were very high. He was never content with success. He always sought to do even better.

It is an extraordinary fact that the most successful fundraisers often have an augury of their future triumphs. They can visualize it. They can feel it. Remember what Schuller said: If you can conceive it, you can achieve it. The big gift, the successful effort, is within your grasp. These great fundraisers know they will be successful. They think it. They know it.

David Ogilvy likes the strange twist. He says that "next to flaring drunkedness and illicit love, nothing appeals to Scotch sentiments so much as having been born to the gutter. I abandoned the cloistered serenity of Oxford and sought my place in the gutter." But that was hardly the case. He set impossible goals, and then met them. He built his one man organization into one of the world's greatest and largest advertising firms.

Norman Vincent Peale is the father of the power of positive thinking. He said: "Plant the seeds of expectation in your mind, cultivate thoughts that anticipate achievement. Believe in yourself as being capable of overcoming all obstacles and weaknesses. If you do this, you will win." When I interviewed John Davis, he was head of the YMCA in Dallas, Texas—one of the strongest associations in the country. Jack is considered by his peers to be one of the most effective fundraisers in the field. He says that if he has any success at all it is because he has high standards and high expectations. He doesn't see how you can really be successful at fundraising if you don't have both of these qualities.

John Miltner feels that you can't really teach a person to have high expectations. It is something that is ingrained. Miltner is vice chancellor of the University of California, Irvine, and immediate past chairman of the largest fundraising society in the world. "In my case, my family really pushed me. I think it's something that's in you or that you get at a very early age. My family just expected a heck of a lot from me. I'm a driven person and I like people who are the same."

All those I interviewed have an unparalleled concern, an unswerving high expectation for the final outcome. They have, as Warren Bennis puts it, an agenda. It is a combination of focus, ambition, and commitment. Add to that: charm, electricity, and aggression. It is intensity joined to dedication. That combination assures success.

If you go into a presentation and are certain you are going to make the sale, you will. If there is any hesitancy, any doubt, you won't. What is required is a compelling and driving desire. It is the kind of determination that motivates enthusiasm and commitment from others.

Russell Conwell attributes his success to always requiring himself to do his best—if only driving a nail straight. There's an interesting difference between the dissatisfaction of a perfectionist and a dissatisfaction with mediocre results. Mediocracy is always acceptable to the mediocre. For the really great fundraisers, good is never good enough.

The world is filled with willing fundraisers. Some are willing to jump hurdles they never thought possible, and the rest willing to let them. In this case, the angels are on the side of those who establish impossible objectives and meet them. They are the inspired fundraisers.

George Bernard Shaw told us that some men see things and ask why, and others dream things that never were, and ask why not. In every way, fundraising is an act of exhilarating discovery. Climbing the highest mountain. Seeking the uncharted course. The fundraiser is a first cousin to the explorer. The final destination is clear. The path, undefined. There are no precise road signs. But the journey and reaching the objective are never in doubt. He may slip, he may fall—but it will always be forward, never backward.

****

4   Moments of Magic

"By working faithfully eight hours a day, you may eventually get to be boss . . . and then work twelve hours a day."
                                                              —Robert Frost

"If you prefer to spend all your spare time growing roses or playing with your children, I shall respect you and I shall like you as a person. But do not complain that you are not successful or not being promoted fast enough. What it takes in this business, or any profession that is worthwhile, is—work, work, work."
                                                              —David Ogilvy

The first thing I remember is the hug. A genuine, gusty bear hug!

His secretary had alerted me about what to expect. She told me that her boss, Vartan Gregorian, has the extraordinary capacity of making everyone feel as if he or she is his best friend. He'll hug you, she cautioned. He hugs everyone. He uses your first name three times in one sentence.

Vartan Gregorian is the impressario, drum major, interpreter, fundraiser, and towering president and chief executive officer of the New York Public Library.

The New York Public Library is a misleading and confusing name, and probably inhibits to some extent its fundraising capacity. The library does indeed receive "public" funds from the city and the state, but it depends each year on $10 million being contributed from the private sector. What Gregorian has done for the library has been called comparable to turning the *Queen Mary* around in a bathtub.

It is one of the most prestigious and important libraries in the world—and the third largest. Its collections are of extraordinary proportions and value. Before Gregorian arrived, the library wasn't dead—but the vital signs were barely visible! The city and state had cut appropriations and the library was selling off assets and closing branches. Today it is a thriving, vital institution twice the size it was when Gregorian arrived. Its endowment has grown from $80 million to $132 million. It has 2750 employees and a value of $120 million in its books and collections—although some are of such important historic significance that a value cannot be placed on them. When Gregorian arrived, the library had an accumulated deficit of $54 million. Today, there is a surplus.

The library is a temple of learning. Eight miles of stacks and 29 million separate items are housed in the research department alone. There was a time when it was open every day for long hours, but during the pre-Gregorian financial crisis, it closed first on Sundays, then on Thursdays, then shortened its hours on other days. No money was available for preservation and irreplaceable books were crumbling. There were no funds for book acquisitions. And the final indignity—the roof leaked! That was only the beginning.

The Fifth Avenue branch, the one best known, extends two whole blocks and is guarded by huge majestic marble lions. It is a monument out of a Cecil B. DeMille movie—opulent interiors, mostly of marble, 530,000 cubic feet in all.

I met with Gregorian in his office on a Saturday. Saturday is his best day because he is more relaxed and works a shorter day—only nine hours.

I walked up wide stone steps that lead to an entrance of huge Corinthian pillars. There's a grand entrance hall, every inch of wall engraved in marble with the names of benefactors. I climbed the massive carved-marble staircase, lighted by chandeliers and lamps on marble posts.

When I enter Gregorian's office, he gets up from his desk to greet me. He doesn't walk. He bounds. His greeting is a combination of a warm handshake and a bear hug. Sort of a gentle wrestling hold! I find myself completely mesmerized. Small wonder men and women queue to give him gifts for the library. Even from the first greeting, his enthusiasm is contagious. He bubbles. He is effervescent.

Hardly your picture of a suave fundraiser, he's short and stout, with wiry hair that seems to stand straight up on his head, as if charged with static. I would have guessed that he and Albert Einstein had the same hairstylist. He is tightly wound. One of the few people I know with clenched hair.

He seems almost out of place. I sat in his office, a lofty impressive sanctum with walls lined with dark green damask, high ceilings, and old paintings of Benjamin Franklin and John Jacob Astor staring down. They passed judgment on our conversation.

And shelves of books—on his desk, on the table, and on the floor. And, as his secretary promised, piles of paper, and papers that weren't in piles.

Gregorian would be considered by some one of the most unlikely candidates for the chief executive's position at the New York Public Library. Here's this Armenian who was born and raised in Iran. Surely the trustees must have wondered whether he could possibly mix, manage, and motivate the scions of New York's most affluential and influential boards. This group, they represented the deepest indigo of blue bloods, the greatest collection of prestige and power in all New York. It was all there, waiting to be ignited by the right spark. It happened, the blaze burst forth—a case of Gregorian combustion!

Andrew Heiskell was chairman of Time, Inc., and chairman of the New York Public Library Board when Gregorian was hired. "We had a search committee and out of the blue, the trustees of the University of Pennsylvania decided not to make Vartan Gregorian the university's president and he just fell into my lap. I took one look at him and it didn't take me more than three minutes to know—this was it." Another board member, Richard Solomon, says: "When Gregorian came, the whole thing fell into place. Before that you thought you were alone, pushing a heavy rock up a hill."

It happened to me, also, and within the first few minutes of our meeting. There was this presence, electrifying and magnetic. He is charged with kinetic energy. He gives the feeling of a time bomb, ready to explode. You sense a passion, an essence of wonder, and a thirst for knowledge and life.

Brooke Astor—Mrs. Vincent Astor—is the effervescent, attractive octogenarian who is honorary chair of the library's board. She says: "If I were asked to give one word for Vartan, I would say it's dynamic. I'm in awe of his fundraising abilities. Absolute awe."

Among the giant fundraisers I interviewed, presence was one characteristic that was consistently and abundantly in evidence. They came in all shapes and sizes, these titans, but they all had riveting presence.

Another characteristic is common in all. Hard work. Arduous hours. For some, a ruthless sacrifice of time. Take Gregorian, for instance. When he was in college, he held down five jobs, took a full course load, and served as president of the Foreign Student's Association. He was always in a hurry. He forced himself to learn English, his sixth language. He says that he did this more quickly by shaving his head. He did this so that he would not be tempted to even go out in the evenings. "I needed only two hours of sleep a night. What makes you tired is your mind and not your body." He says that now that he is older, he requires more sleep. Now he needs three or four hours a night.

He works 14 hours a day, six days a week. He goes non-stop. Morning, noon, night. His chairman says that Gregorian spreads this enthusiasm to others and that his optimism is infectious. Some fundraisers say: It can't be done, or maybe it can be done. The inspired ones say: Everything can be done. For some, there are always doubts, questions, reservations, and hand-wringing. To the inspired ones, such as Gregorian, the attitude, no matter what the challenge: Sure we can do it. In fact, that's a typical comment of Gregorian's. He never says no. On his tombstone I would chisel "Sure We Can Do It—But Now It May Take Longer."

"I have a weakness," Gregorian told me. "I have many weaknesses. I should be able to take time off. The cemetery is filled with people who could not take time off. But somehow, I just can't seem to manage it. A day here and a day there, but seldom much more. My work consumes me. I love it.'' I find that among the great fundraisers, something is always attainable beyond ''best.'' And anything less, is simply not good enough. They say only three ingredients are needed to be a successful fundraiser: Hard work, hard work, and hard work.

But this appears to be common among successful men and women in all disciplines. Sarah Caldwell is the world renowned musical director of Boston's Opera Company. She says: ''I love what I do. I can work for days without sleep because I get so caught up with every detail. Once in a while, when everything is just right, there's a moment of magic.'' People can live on moments of magic. And that's it. Those moments of magic. All of us in fundraising can identify with that. Those precious moments of total exhilaration. You've just secured a large gift. You've been working on it for months. Your strategy was nearly perfect. Best of all, the donor is excited, and grateful to you. You did it. You know that through you, you will be changing lives. And saving lives. Those moments, those moments are pure magic.

Dr. Alton Ochsner, founder of the Ochsner Clinic, trained Michael DeBakey at Tulane. DeBakey is perhaps the preeminent surgeon in the world. Ochsner says that DeBakey is one of those individuals who shows you can accomplish anything if you put in the hours. The 80-year-old DeBakey maintains a tireless pace. He rises at five o'clock in the morning. Every day. He performs seven to nine procedures every day at Methodist, the teaching hospital for Baylor College of Medicine. His normal day ends sometime after 11:00 p.m.

The consummate fundraisers all seem to have the kinds of values, work ethics, and resolve that propel them to greatness. I've known a lot of men and women in our field who are TGIM people—Thank God It's Monday, I can go to the office!

I feel that work has gotten a bum rap in recent years, particularly from people who do not like to work. The word "workaholic" has a meaning which implies drunk on work. Or consider the term "Protestant Ethic." At one time, that was a perfectly suitable explanation for the economic behavior of a historical people—but today, it exists almost solely as a pejorative term. The great fundraisers take immense joy in their work. For them, their work often seems to be more pleasurable than even being with good friends. And for many, after two or three days of splendid vacation, they are itching to get back in the harness. Helping to save lives or change lives isn't work—it's sheer fun. Charles Steinmetz, the genius inventor, said that he had succeeded in getting his actual work down to 30 minutes a day—which left him 18 uninterrupted hours for engineering and sheer fun.

Napoleon Hill is the author of a number of books, one of which, *Think and Grow Rich*, is among the top ten best selling books ever printed. He says: "I've carefully studied men with the object of determining why some achieve noteworthy success while others with just as much ability do not get ahead. It seems significant that every person I've observed applies the principle of rendering more service than that for which he is paid, was holding a better position and receiving more pay than those who merely performed sufficient service to 'get by' with." The real success stories belong to those who are willing to do more than anticipated, willing to do more than they get paid for, willing to go the extra mile, willing to work obsessively hard.

Dr. Joyce Brothers says that when she refers to high achievers and uses the term "hard work" she means: "Working at top capacity for 70 or 80 hours, or more, every week—loving their work until it becomes a driving passion, and devoting all of their waking hours to thinking, planning, and striving toward goals which others consider impossible. Total commitment." Charles B. Thornton was the man who built Litton Industries. He got up at four o'clock in the morning so he could be in the office by five: "You live it, eat it, sleep it, breathe it."

No rule for success will work if you won't. Dr. Milton J. Murray is among the select circle considered to be titans in our field. He says: "I am a hard worker, and I love it. My dad used to set the pace. He'd go to work early in the morning, then go back to the office at night. I think that made a tremendous impression on me and set the pattern for my own life. But I love it." That seems to be the key to the great fundraisers. They are not working hard, they are having fun. The only double Nobel laureate, Linus Pauling, says he won the Nobel Prize in chemistry by "simply having fun."

To the inspired fundraiser, work is his essence. Through it, he discovers the marvel of his own human spirit. He becomes himself. He fulfills himself. I am not suggesting this for everyone. Not all are willing to make the sacrifice. But if you really desire to secure the big gift, if you really want to be at the top in your profession, if you are really willing to go through the pain and agony of being your most effective self, you have to go a little berserk. You make a giant leap in consciousness and personal growth and self-esteem. And you become delightfully delirious. You become utterly absorbed in another world and your work. The exhilaration exceeds the exhaustion.

An old axiom says that he who rolls up his sleeves, seldom loses his shirt. Milton Murray says that he usually takes work home with him at night. He manages to get in an extra hour or two that way. It's second nature to him. He is one with Henry James that our work is our mania. We give all we have. Our objective is our passion and our passion is our task.

Jim Bowers says that the willingness and drive to work hard is probably ingrained. "There are some men and women who are simply driven, hard working in everything they do. For some, it may be developed but I think that those who have this trait probably have been that way from the very first day they started working. And in fundraising, it takes a tremendous amount of hard work to get the job done." He goes on to say: "Anyone who wants an eight-to-five job should not go into this business. I think that I am a pretty organized person and it simply takes more hours than that. And then there are all the evenings and weekends. There's all the business of running the operation, making the contacts, returning the phone calls, the endless but necessary meetings, and the required socializing. And then there's all the essential reading. There's no end to it and it just takes a lot of hours. I imagine I average somewhere between 60 and 80 hours a week. I don't know whether this is right or wrong. I just don't think I could do my job in anything less. I take work home with me and I work on weekends."

The great fundraisers always seem to pass the same litmus test: Their profession is not merely a higher calling, it is missionary work. They are not merely competitive, they are driven to win. They do not simply work hard, they work relentlessly. It is possible that persistence and hard work are the only original and surviving contributions we make to this world. Everything else is given to us. Health, strength, intelligence—these are mostly inherent. But tenacity, diligence, and hard work are elements we can add.

One of the great men in our business, Robert Duncan, said that hard work is one of the most important criterion of the effective fundraiser. Duncan felt that a fundraiser should be assiduous. Assiduous! Now that is a word you hardly hear nowadays. But it is ever-present in those who are successful in our field. Tom Peters says: "It's hanging in long after others have gotten bored and given up. It's refusing to leave well enough alone. It means that anything less than the best you can imagine really bothers you, maybe keeps you awake at night. It usually means sticking your neck out, daring to give your best shot, and working beyond anything considered normal limits."

Father Hesburgh says: "I am an evening person. The truth of the matter is, I don't do very well in the morning. I think each one of us runs on his own clock. It is not unusual for me to come back to the office after dinner and dictate until three or four in the morning. I do that pretty regularly. I'm not proud of that and I don't recommend it for others. It just is the way that I work. And I work that way seven days a week. Time is precious. It is our most precious commodity. I can't stand to waste it. I do whatever I have to do. Someone once asked me how much sleep I need. I need as much as I get. You do what you have to do."

Malcolm S. Forbes recently reported the secret of his success. "Unswerving dedication to the job, unrelenting hard work, long hours without complaint, and a father who left me over $100 million!" But not everyone is as fortunate. In a recent article in the *Wall Street Journal*, Dr. Thomas Stanley wrote about America's typical millionaire. How did he get to where he is, this millionaire? "The key word, alas, is work. The rich are a painfully disciplined lot. Those 75-hour work weeks aren't in vain. These people are some of the happiest in the world." We get the same joy in our field, not necessarily in a monetary way. But we are busy saving lives and changing lives. That is our great high. That is what gives us exhilaration and strength. George Gallup, Jr., has co-authored a superb book called *Great American Success Stories*. In it he says that the typical executive puts in 63-hour work weeks. A few really top achievers work as many as 90 to 100 hours a week.

Of course. I know, I know! It takes more. It takes strategic savvy, creative communications, and mighty motivational skills. All that and more. But the greatest of these may simply be hard work. Some are willing to work eight hours a day, some even less. For those who work 12 hours, they get an extra four hours on their competition. Each week, that's a whole half week more than those who are willing to settle for less. An extra 20 to 25 weeks each year.

The high achievers probably succeed because they are single-mindedly devoted and committed to achieving their objective. As noted, some would refer to these men and women as workaholics. But that implies an illness. If you are doing what you want to do more than anything else in the world, why should you punish yourself by cutting down on the things that make you most happy? The really great fundraisers seem to enjoy the stress of coping with difficulties. They appear to be attracted to what one medical researcher refers to as "the call of controlled risk." They seek it because they are filled with energy—feeling more vital when they are active and working hard. Scientific research data substantiates the case that stress and hard work help assure a healthier person.

Life at the top of the mountain can be rewarding, exhilarating. But it's tough. A slippery, difficult climb. A recent survey of chief executive officers of the top 100 companies in the country indicate that these men and women average 57 hours a week at the office. In addition, they spend an average of ten hours a week working at home. That adds up to 13 extra 40-hour work weeks—or three extra months each year for these top executives. Robert Schuller says: "Many people get hung up on the word 'talent.' They think it's something you were born with. I contend that frequently talent is something you acquire, like experience or wisdom. It can be developed through hard work, like studying. Frequently, talent and skill are spelled: W—O—R—K."

The great fundraisers move on an even keel, but most of them tend to be hyperkinetic. What seems common throughout is that they have the persistence to strive for mastery and the drive to excel. They seem to work at a pace that can best be termed as constructive tension.

Phyllis Allen says that she works from 7:30 in the morning until 7:30 at night. "And then I pretty regularly take a briefcase home and work!" Joel P. Smith is retired vice president for development at Stanford University. He says that it is obvious that effective fundraisers must work hard. "We occasionally read or hear about extraordinary people who accomplish phenomenal things with very little effort and in very little time. But I have never run into one. The only truly productive people I know are deliberately industrious." George Engdahl fits the pattern: "I am a driven man. I thoroughly enjoy the work I am doing. I always take work home and I work weekends at home. But somehow it never seems like work. It is sheer fun. I am devoted to it and I love it." There it is again, the feeling that it is not work at all—it is fun. That's your great fundraiser.

Father Hesburgh says: "I work hard and I expect my staff to work hard. I feel a sense of dedication and willingness to stay up all night if necessary to get the job done. And I've done that many times." The great fundraisers set a clear example for those who work with them. To keep up, they, too, must work hard.

At times, when doing the research, when handling the minutia and details required in this job, fundraising can be compared to running a marathon—both exhausting and exhilarating. The task can be laborious and deadly dull. But when you finally reach your objective, the taste of victory is worth it all.

These great fundraisers give sacrificially of themselves. Their time. Their sleep. Even their families suffer. Year after year. In a sense, they leverage their lives to the great ministry of fundraising. There is faith. There is sacrifice. And the never-ending, devoted giving of time.

Nietzsche said that you must never trust an idea that you come upon while relaxing! Vince Lombardi had his own way of putting it. "Everytime a football player goes out to ply his trade, he's got to play from the ground up—from the soles of his feet right up to his head. Every inch of him has to play. Some guys play with their heads, and sure, you need to be smart to be number one in anything you try. But most important, you've got to play with your heart. If you're lucky enough to find a guy with a lot of head and a lot of heart, he's never going to come off the field second. I always tell my football players that the only way to lick the other team is outwork them. They may be smarter than you, they may be faster, and they may even have better plays. But if you outwork them, you are bound to win. Hard work is everything."

I have heard it many times, from those who seem to know. They claim that anyone who works beyond normal hours or who takes a briefcase home is not well organized and should not be held in high esteem. A pitiful back-bowed, over-worked soul destined for purgatory with a bulging briefcase of grant proposals and case statements to be completed. But there's too much evidence against this theory, too much substantiation for the ebullience and ecstasy that comes with hard work.

I confess to being a rollicking, willing, uncontrollable work-aholic myself. I love it. Aha! Now you understand my bias. I am a card-carrying workaholic and proud of it. Those I consider to be the great ones in the field share the same characteristic. No, it doesn't mean that if you work hard and long hours, you will necessarily be successful. And I know all about the admonition to "work smarter, not harder." But the really hard working men and women, always seem to be the ones that end up owning Boardwalk and Park Place. And they're always studying, preparing, and practicing. They believe in the axiom: Practice doesn't make perfect, perfect practice makes perfect.

Roger Smith, CEO of General Motors, has a response to the work smarter, not harder impudency. "I've always been impressed by those guys who work a seven and eight hour day and I think it's a great idea. I'm not certain they ever get very near the top at General Motors. As for me, I somehow have never seemed to be able to get my life and my work that well organized. I've always had to work 16 hours a day, seven days a week. I love it." In the words of Kipling, he ". . . fills the unforgiving minute with sixty seconds worth of exhilarating run."

Sometimes we in the development business feel that we are the only ones drowning in an ocean of work. I have felt it myself. But I find that in virtually every field, every endeavor worth working at, in every significant mission, the professionals have the same complaint. Too much to do and not enough time in which to do it. The ocean is so large and my row boat is so small.

Leonard Bernstein felt the same need for more hours in a day. Once he recited an ode he had written to his orchestra:

> Love one another, and sing while you play.
> And be good to each other, even while I'm away,
> And so forward, my hearties, with courage and cheer,
> To a season with 98 weeks in the year.

Here's the important lesson. Hard work is essential, but it must have focus. You cannot be like the man on the Los Angeles freeway who says to his wife: "Don't worry that we're lost, honey. We're making good time." There must be an ultimate objective, a well-defined and time-phased schedule, and a dazzling program that makes you reach beyond anything you thought possible. You must combine all of this with the willingness to work hard.

Inertia and apathy enervates. Activity and hard work energize. They energize the fundraiser and assure the success of the program. In some circles, people have come to sneer at success, if it requires hard work and sacrifice. Expecting successful results by giving less than your full measure is the most senseless form of unrealistic hope.

Jim Bowers says: "If you're going to be a star performer, you can't sit back and relax. You have to work and make sacrifices. And what you'll find is that it's not work—it's fun. If you are a leader, you better lead—and you lead by example. You have to motivate staff, volunteers and donors, and let them know what you want them to see. Get them to do what you want them to do. This is not an easy business. You can't run it from nine-to-five. Most of all, it takes hard work." George Engdahl said that he never thinks of the hours he puts in as being work. He says that it's not work, it's recreation. Just plain fun.

Herman B. Wells was for years the highly esteemed president of Indiana University. He said: "Work like hell because the job deserves it, needs it, and is worth it. Universities have been injured more by a lazy staff than by incompetent or dictatorial ones. It takes long hours, thoughtful practice at the trade, and hard work." Dr. Bruce Heilman has just retired as president of the University of Richmond. Before he arrived, the board was talking about bankruptcy proceedings and the city had just condemned a major portion of the school's facilities as being uninhabitable. During his extraordinary tenure, the school evolved into one of the great small universities in the country. Heilman says: "There's never been a time when there isn't something to do. That's been true all my life. There's always so much in front of me that must be done. If you slow down, someone is going to pull the chair from under you. If you're doing well, you've got to keep running. Work with all you've got, that's the key."

When told he was a genius, Paderewski said: "Before I was a genius, I was a drudge." Nothing worthwhile comes easily. Half effort does not produce half results—it produces no results. For the fundraiser, work, hard work, continuous work is the only way to accomplish great achievements. You need not worry about genius. You need not worry about being clever. Just work.

It is important to dream—sublime to dream and work. Faith is important. But faith with work is mightier. Desire is important. But desire and work are invincible.

In a recent *New Yorker* cartoon, a frazzled and weary school teacher is climbing out of a classroom window to end it all. One first grader turns to the other and explains: "Teacher burn-out." Yes, we hear a lot about burn-out these days. Those relentless hours I speak of, I assume that they can lead to burn-out. But somehow, among these prodigious fundraisers I spoke with and have quoted, no evidence of burn-out appears. Not the slightest. On the contrary, their lives seem to be filled with the zest that comes with a full and joyous spirit. Engravened with the same joyous theme of the Flying Tigers in China—undermanned, overworked, and successful!

There is a nobility about hard work. Even the weariness it leaves is exhilarating, intoxicating. The long days and long nights—all are worth the price. Results and success. To win requires hard work and iron resolution. And supreme effort and self-sacrifice. The power of work in the sense of duty brings no greater joy in life.

Life is an unending succession of opportunities. Work is opportunity in disguise. "I can't do it," never accomplishes anything. The Vartan Gregorian "Sure, we can do it" makes things happen.

Men and women of talent—willing to sacrifice and work—make the discoveries, write the books, win the campaigns, and order the world. Work touches the heart with fire. And instills zeal in life. It provides the fundraiser purpose and pride. New actions. New aspirations. New efforts. New vision. All these are due less to genius than to perseverance and determination. The successful fundraiser is the one who gives himself to his work—body and soul.

I don't necessarily recommend this uphill, rocky, slippery road for everyone. You have to determine whether it is worth the sacrifice of soul and the suffering of mind. Along with David Ogilvy, if you decide to take an easier course and grow your roses and play with your children—I shall be your friend and respect you. In fact, you may be the wise one. I've spoken many times on the subject of what makes an inspired fundraiser and I point out that in my judgment, hard work is one of the most important characteristics. It never fails that after the presentation, some men and women—almost militant—come to the podium to argue the point. I concede, they may be the wise ones. Each person has to decide whether the time and the agony are worth the compromise it makes in one's life. But I am convinced that hard work pays immense dividends, makes the difference, distinguishes the winners from the also-rans.

I am told that the world is divided into three types: Those who are immovable, those who are movable, and those who move. Hard work is the mightiest and most powerful force on earth. The indefatigable fundraisers will win the campaigns, secure the large gifts, and assure the perpetuity of their institutions.

****

5   Can Do

"If I have been able to do more and have seen further, it is because I have been able to stand on the shoulders of giants."

—Isaac Newton

"Pigmys placed on the shoulders of giants see more than the giants themselves."

—Lucan

I wish you could have been with me to watch him work the crowd.

It was a small gathering of friends, alumni, parents, and corporate executives held at the plush Metropolitan Club in New York City. These were men and women who had made major gifts to the University of Richmond. Dr. Bruce Heilman, president of the university, had asked me to join him for the luncheon honoring and recognizing these benefactors—about 50 all together. Heilman filled the room with his presence. In his assured, quiet way, he towered. He seemed to demonstrate supreme self-confidence—as they say, "like a Baptist with four aces!" But it was a calm, subtle confidence.

There was a warm, fond greeting for each person, and the most beguiling smile imaginable. He was prepared for this meeting and he knew his people well. I watched him "bend" the group. It was a delight to watch this great one in action. In each case, there was a personal inquiry, a comment about a child's work at the university, a concern about a person's recent illness. Even a comment about one family's pet dog. He didn't miss a thing.

After lunch, he spoke. The sparks flew. It was not of electrical storm proportions—that's not his style as a speaker. But an unquestionable new energy filled the room. The group was galvanized. It was a superb presentation.

What was it about this man that made such a difference? It was partly his presence. When he spoke, he seemed ten feet tall. It was not an emotional speech. No arms flailing. But it was highly compelling. He spoke about the needs of the university and his vision for the future. And he laid it on the line emphatically. He told the group that funds were necessary to continue the work of the school and fulfill its destiny. I have a feeling that in his obituary someone will write ". . . and he asked for the order!"

When the meeting was over, Bruce Heilman and I walked down Fifth Avenue toward the University Club. He said to me: "I think self-confidence is everything. It may perhaps be the most important ingredient in fundraising. I don't see how a person can really go after a large gift if he doesn't have the confidence that he'll get it. A lot of factors come into play, but he better have self-confidence." He told me that he is actually an introvert, that being in a group like today's luncheon is not easy for him. "Do you understand the difference? I'm an introvert but I have a great deal of self-confidence. I know that I am the right person at this time in the history of the university. That helps me do whatever needs to be done."

Bruce Heilman was born in Ballordsville, Kentucky, a village of 65 people. Six decades later, Ballordsville is just the same size. He attended Campbellsville College, a school of 200 students. "I have thought about this before and as far as I know, I believe that I am the only one from our town who ever went to college. I was the only one from our family who went." This was, by the way, a phenomenon which was common among the great fundraisers I interviewed. Virtually all were raised in small communities and attended small schools. I believe that this fascinating coincidence has much to do with the manner in which they bring dedication, determination, and drive to their fundraising endeavors.

Before Heilman arrived as president, the University of Richmond was near bankruptcy and four of its dormitories were condemned by the Richmond Health Authority. During his 15-year tenure, endowment grew from $800,000 to $200 million. Over $75 million has been raised and spent for new buildings. A $50 million campaign was completed two years ahead of schedule and immediately followed with a $55 million campaign—which will be completed successfully ahead of schedule. Today, they raise in excess of ten million dollars a year.

It's a remarkable transformation, from a school that nearly went out of business to one which is now considered one of the very finest small universities in the nation. Bruce Heilman is given the major credit for making this happen. He, in turn, says that his self-confidence played the major role—that and being in the right place at the right time. It was a felicitious combination.

Dr. Matina Horner is president of Radcliffe College. She talks about how important the proper attitude can be. There was extreme poverty in her home, but when friends came to visit, "we were always wonderful hosts. There were never complaints, never a feeling of being sorry for ourselves. We were positive, and reflected in a bigger, more overall attitude of positiveness. That same feeling has affected everything I do." Her father was a street vendor, bur Horner speaks about how extremely well read he was. "He could quote from many of the great philosophers. He was the most self-actualized man I know, very wise. We were poor. But what I remember about being poor was never feeling poor." She says: "All my life, I've worked hard for whatever I've wanted. My attitude has always been that where there is a will, there's a way." She feels that this is the factor which has driven her to get the very best out of people. "I have supreme self-confidence in what I am doing. My job is to provide a supportive environment for talented people to self-maximize."

Bruce Heilman says: "Self-confidence is about at the top of the list for me. If that fails me at any point, I know I'm not going to get the gift. I've lost. You have got to have the feeling you can do it. If you move forward with a claim to the space, people will make room for you. In fundraising, self-confidence is essential. You've got to know that you're the leader. You've got to believe you can raise the money, you can motivate the prospect, you can get the big gift. Without confidence in yourself, you won't do it." A development team and staff must think of itself as winners. Prospective donors will seldom entrust their funds to an institution or people who do not exude legitimate, quiet pride and confidence in the institution's accomplishments and ability to produce significant results.

Frank Lloyd Wright is very likely the high priest of ego and in his typically overstated fashion, he said: "I chose honest arrogance over hypocritical humility!" George Engdahl puts it differently. "I think anyone who's successful in this business has a strong ego. It's called a healthy ego and by that I think they mean the kind of personality where you have a great deal of confidence in yourself. You have the feeling that you have your act all together. There are enough times when not everything goes the way you would like it and you have to have a strong ego and personality to overcome that."

For some in our profession, the fear of failure consumes. Fear is one of the most difficult problems we face. So much of fundraising is selling yourself, putting your own ego on the line. I once heard a great salesman say that if you are really good, you are probably going to fail at least half of the time. In our business, rejection comes with the territory. But Schuller says that when a program does not succeed, it is never the fault of the fundraiser. The fault lies with the dream, the vision, the plans. He says there are no poor fundraisers, only poor and ill-conceived plans, "only unexceptional and unexciting ideas."

One day, Charlie Brown was talking to his friend, Linus, about the pervasive sense of inadequacy he feels all the time. "You see, Linus," Charlie bemoaned, "it goes all the way back to the beginning. The moment I was born and set foot on the stage of life, they took one look at me and said, 'not right for the part.' " Does this mean that some are doomed from the beginning? That the most important talents and traits are inherent and cannot be learned? Charles Beacham, former chief executive of Ford, thinks so: "Once a guy is over 21, you never really change his style or his habits. You may think you can, but his self-image is locked in."

But I am convinced that this need not be the case. I feel certain that self-assurance can be learned, but only with discipline and dedication. Confidence comes from knowledge. I have seen dazzling examples. If you know you can do it, you will have the confidence necessary when the stakes are the highest and you are called on for your greatest effort. Tom Landry, football coach of the Dallas Cowboys, says: "If you really know your job, you will do well when you get out on the field. You've got to think about the positive elements all of the time, because once you start thinking about the negative possibilities . . . it drastically reduces your chance of achieving your best. Anyone can be a winner if he wants it enough, strives for it hard enough, actively seeks it out by learning all he can and working with all of his strength. Confidence makes the difference."

Some have to really work at being confident. You do all you can, with all you have. Trust your own instincts and draw deep from your subconscious to develop new ideas. It helps to work at it when the mind is relaxed. Disregard the past. Create your own brilliant precedents. Perhaps the philosopher-jazz musician Thelonious Monk was on target when he said: "Sometimes I play things I never heard myself."

All this business about being the best in the field, about being the most successful, the inspired fundraisers—it serves a purpose in establishing a model but it does put emphasis in the wrong place. We strive, all of us, for excellence. The Greeks called it *arete*—virtue. It means functioning as you're supposed to function. Not necessarily being the best in the field, but being the very best you can possibly be. Sam Snead said: "Forget your opponents; always play against yourself and par."

It seems to be axiomatic in this business, if you refuse to accept anything but the best, you most often get it! If you are willing to accept less than the best, you'll get that, too. And that's the point. If we all work to our highest potential, do all we are capable of doing, we would literally astound ourselves.

General George S. Patton, no shrinking violet, said it well: "The most vital quality a successful person can possess is self-confidence—utter, complete and bumptious. You can have doubts about your good looks, about your intelligence, about your self-control, but to win, you must have no doubts about your ability." Bruce Heilman does not fear failure. "I only fear the slowing up of the engine inside of me which keeps pounding, saying: 'Keep going, someone must be on top, why not you?'" It can be said of Heilman that he is the sort of man who would go after Moby Dick with a row boat, a harpoon, and a jar of tartar sauce!

The great fundraisers all have presence. That's difficult to define. But you can feel it, sense it, see it. It's poise, self-assurance, confidence (there's that word again!), a certain cachet. These men and women, they fill a room.

"I am convinced," says Bruce Heilman, "that you can make yourself into about anything you want to be. That's the way you look, the way you act, and the way you dress. And that gets back to the business of self-confidence. I am not an extrovert, but I like people. I make myself do what needs to be done. I don't enjoy parties and one social event after another, but that's my job. And I totally enjoy the requirements of my job. I play an important role at the university. Presence is crucial to fulfilling my responsibility. It is something that I consciously work at."

All those I consider to be the best in the business agree that being physically attractive is not important. Not a lot can be done about that. You're dealt a certain hand, and you do the best you can. George Engdahl says: "I think having presence is terribly important. By that I don't mean being physically attractive. That's not the same as having presence. It means being able to stand out in a positive way. I thank people in our business have to be put together well and dress well—and something I feel is extremely important, they have to look physically fit. We have control over the things that I have mentioned."

"A fundraiser should look and act a certain way. It is expected." That's Bruce Heilman speaking again. "Our image is extremely important. There is a certain expectation that you will act and look as you should. I suppose anyone is allowed to be different and do their own thing. That's their privilege. But not in our business."

What is it then, this elusive quality called presence? "Being pretty has nothing to do with it," says Jim Bowers. It's how you are groomed, how you dress, and your facial expression. Whatever it is, some people have it and some don't. Persons with a commanding presence seem to take over when they enter a room. It's a subtle sort of thing which just happens."

When I spoke about presence to those I interviewed, few took a stab at trying to actually define it. In most cases, they tended to list the factors which contribute to it in a positive way. Enthusiasm was mentioned often. Prospects are persuaded more by the depth of your conviction than the height of your logic. They are won more by your own enthusiasm than any documentation you can offer.

Fundraising isn't what it used to be. It never was. It takes humor, gusto, kinetic energy and the unrelenting power to endure. And it takes a sense of humor, a battered, but happy warrior.

But one of the chief ingredients for a successful fundraiser is enthusiasm. Listen to W. Clement Stone, one of the great philanthropists of our country. If anyone has encountered a range of fundraising types, he has. He began as a newsboy on the sidewalks of Chicago and built the largest insurance company of its kind in the world. He built an empire, and he did it by first "discovering" and then generating enthusiasm in his salespeople. He told me once he believed that the major component which is absolutely essential for a successful and effective fundraiser is enthusiasm.

"What do you mean by enthusiasm?" I asked. I have learned with Stone that there is always a response!

He told me about the derivation of the word: "Enthusiasm comes from two Greek words and it really gives you the funda-

mental and original meaning. First, there's *theos* which means
God. The rest of the word means 'within you'. God within
you.''

That says it all.

The really great fundraisers must have a vision—and the
courage to advance the dream. They also need the resolve to
pursue it and to overcome any and all resistance. It's what Clark
Kerr, former chancellor of the University of California, calls:
''A willingness both to endure and inflict pain along the way.''

The great fundraisers are without limit in their vision.
They transmit it in a dramatic and compelling manner. There is
a celebration of the creation and cause of their institutions and
its mission. They are audacious enough to dream and to share
the dream. But it's more than just dreaming. They turn ideas
into action. These great fundraisers, they make lightning strike
the things they care about. Their vision and enthusiasm is
infectious. They know, too, that positive thoughts make positive things happen. Lives are changed by the ''can do'' attitude,
and not the ''can't.''

John Gardner says that the times cry out for change, but
we've resisted with unholy stubbornness. But the really great
fundraisers exhibit uncontrolled abandonment to the most brilliant of visions. The fundraiser can create miracles with the right
mission and vision. But vision comes only with an unquestionable and unquestioning belief in the mission of your institution.
Says Bruce Heilman: ''If you really believe in your cause, if you
really believe in your institution, you can raise funds. You've
got to feel that your organization makes a difference. A unique
difference. If you don't really believe that, you'll never be a
great fundraiser. If you are an average fundraiser and you don't
believe in your institution, you could have been a really great
fundraiser if you did believe.''

It is significant that when most of those I interviewed
spoke about the vision and their own personal covenant with

the mission of their institution, they related this to their own spiritual values. It is also significant and fascinating to note that virtually all of those interviewed emerged from a culture and environment shaped by religious values. Not all are church-goers now, but there was a deep-rooted spiritual quality in their formative years. I had not thought about it before but there has to be a direct relationship between success and this moral order, this spiritual foundation, that propels these fund-raisers forward.

This background molds soft metal into steel. It creates the foundation of their work and ethic. Their sensitivity to people. Their self-confidence. Their deep commitment to the organization.

William Blake said that great things happen when men and mountains meet. Brian Lurie is emphatic on the matter. "I don't want to say that a secular person can't bring a commitment. But I think it really takes a spiritual background in order to be an effective fundraiser. It's almost axiomatic."

How can I be so certain. Surely, legions of effective fund-raisers without soaring spiritual values or early church influences are far better than just competent, generating significant funds for their institutions. Of course! But the high flyers I spoke with all had strong religious faith or spiritual dimensions that were part of their early home life. It appeared to be virtually a *sine qua non* of the top people. I suspect that the deep spiritual grounding in their early home life provided a sense of security and self-esteem that enabled them to take giant leaps forward. A skyrocket of faith. And it likely, also, gave them the courage and comfort to assume risks.

Robert L. Payton is the former president of Exxon Educa-tion Foundation. He points out that modern philanthropy has lost its conscious sense of the traditions and values of true charity. "Today, policymakers are further removed from the recipients of charity and philanthropy than was the case in simpler and smaller societies of the past. As giving and receiving became increasingly systematized and specialized, organizational values replaced personal ones. Detached as they are now from religion, charity and philanthropy lose their place to value-neutral terms like 'grant making' and 'contributions.' "

And now, another assumption as to why the great fund-raisers seem to have spiritual values and a positive environment of religion threaded through their background. This environment imposes a personal obligation on them to relieve the suffering of others, by prompt and positive action. The concept of charity comes out of a religious context.

Many will quarrel with this but if you are not in this business because you have a strong tug of religious and spiritual consciousness, your fundraising work will not be operating on full cylinders. I believe it's true that without these spiritual values our work becomes less of a personal and unrelenting obligation and dedication, and more impersonal and untouching. Mumbo jumbo, you say. Then talk with any of the great people in the field about the spiritual and religious background they bring to their work and their code of values. Speak also to the benefactors, those who give the largest gifts. The evidence is clear that they respond to the fundraiser with the greatest missionary zeal and the most pervasive spiritual qualities.

What then does one do? On his death bed, a priest asked Henry Thoreau whether he had made his peace with God. He replied: "I was not aware we had quarreled." We bring to this business what we are, whatever that is. We had no control over the factors which shaped and molded us. I only report what I felt and what I found. Don't slay the messenger! Every one of the great ones I interviewed—there were no exceptions—came from a religious background.

What do you do if this is not part of your background? To be the best you can, to reach your optimum effectiveness, to be a really high achiever, you must begin now a phase of self-discovery. It may take a long time, but it is possible to change and to improve.

No matter how long we've been at this business, we can grow. Isolation and study. Search and solitude. Introspection. A grinding and continuing self-challenging examination. The great fundraisers feel this accountability every day. They are driven by it. There are those days, we all have them, that are filled with the heavy sense of failure. But we know there is always a new day, a better day, better than the one before.

****

6   Between the 40-yard lines

"Make three correct guesses consecutively and you will establish a reputation for being an expert."
—Lawrence Peter, The Peter Principle

"Anyone who has a bull by the tail knows five or six things more than someone who hasn't."
—Mark Twain

There is the sense of disciplined order and uncommonly good taste in equal measure. That's the dominant impression when you enter the office of Jim Bowers. Everything has a place, and everything is in superb style. Those who are close to Jim know that he is compulsive about the organization of his work and in doing things with a certain panache. In the field of fundraising, he is as good as they come.

Jim is well-ordered, some might say neat to a fault. He is not alone in this regard. According to Neil Welch, once a top field chief in the FBI, his boss J. Edgar Hoover was a man to whom neatness counted a great deal. He was down right manic on the matter of neatness. Welch tells the story of the day Hoover received a memo with such messy margins that he wrote back: "Watch the borders." His subordinates took this order literally and immediately dispatched scores of agents to keep their eyes on the areas bordering Mexico and Canada.

Bowers brings an understanding of fundraising unlike most in the business. He has been vice president of three colleges and universities, head of a major city symphony, executive officer of the New York Public Library, a consultant with a national fundraising firm, and now heads the foundation at Scripps Memorial Hospitals in La Jolla, California. He has sat at virtually every seat around the table!

When he first came to Scripps, what modest fundraising was done at the institution was handled primarily by the very efficient secretary of the administrator. Today, the hospital raises about ten million dollars each year. That's probably more than any community hospital in the country. They have just announced a campaign for $100 million, the largest objective ever undertaken by a community hospital. Anyone who knows Jim will bet it will be successful.

I compare him to the magnificent pipe organ at the old Enright Theater where I grew up in Pittsburgh's East Liberty— it had three decks, fifty stops, and a pride of pedals under the bench. When Jim Bowers wants a special trick or technique, it's there!

He was born and raised in Beaver Falls, a small western Pennsylvania community of 18,000. He did his undergraduate work at Geneva College with an enrollment of 800 students. As I noted earlier, virtually all the great fundraisers I interviewed were either born or reared in a small community and took their undergraduate work at a small college. There is no real explanation. But it doesn't mean that you can't be a giant in this business if you're from Cleveland, Ohio. Jim has a theory on the subject: "The people I respect in this field have all pretty much come from small communities and have attended small colleges. Most of them are generalists in the field, and I think that a small college engenders this. I also think that a love and concern for people—which is terribly important in our business—is generated in a small community."

He is compulsive and intense. "I think most really effective fundraisers are," says Bowers. He also has a highly developed sense of curiosity. He probes and explores everything that concerns his work, his prospects, and life around him. He's like the diamond-cutter, who studies and turns his stone this way and that, seeking the precise cut for the perfect jewel.

His life is compartmentalized and tightly organized. One of his associates told me you could perform open-heart surgery on Jim Bowers' desk! And aesthetics are important to him, how things look and how things sound. He is a keen observer. Nothing escapes his scrutiny.

He has a computer in his office, but I have never seen him use it. I honestly didn't think he knew how until I saw him flick it on the other day. Nothing is too minor for his purview. He doesn't really need his IBM—he puts everything into his mental computer for future reference. And when it comes to prospects, he forgets nothing. Absolutely nothing! He possesses a facile mind, a many-splendored imagination, and an utter contempt for the ordinary. There is superior intellect and a stupefying capacity for hard, concentrated work. He is one of those deep sea fish that can function best under enormous pressure. In fact, he creates his own deep sea!

He suffers greatly from the same malady as most I interviewed. He feels his work is never done, his task never completed. Something can always be done better, more effectively. Not a tranquil life, that sort of attitude—but most of the great ones in this business seem to have it. Most often, "best effort" just isn't good enough.

Like Bowers, most of the great ones in the business are fanatical about details. Not office mechanics and the minutia of fundraising—they tend to abhor these things. But they do understand that really great fundraising takes place between the 40-yard lines. That's how you go over goal. And that means hard work and scrupulous attention to details. The secret of successful fundraising is very likely the ability to do the common details uncommonly well.

Vartan Gregorian calls it a flaw, but doesn't really mean it! "I have a great weakness that I can do nothing about. What I mean is that I know every detail. I couldn't survive or handle this position any other way. I feel it gives me an edge. Even minor things, every detail. Maybe I shouldn't. But I'm pleased to know that Harvard has said that my type of management is now in vogue. I do a lot of walking around. I know all of my library branches. I know all of my people. I know them by name and I know their families. I have 1800 employees and staff. I know them all intimately. I couldn't survive any other way." He also knows every single major prospect. He knows everything about them. Nothing escapes his mania for detail. Great fundraisers, they are made of that sort of stuff.

For some, those who are willing to accept less than the very best, details are boring. But details aren't boring. Boring is boring Charles Dickens said: "I should never have made my success in life if I had not bestowed upon the least thing I have ever undertaken the same attention and care that I have bestowed upon the greatest." The inspired ones in our business agree with that thesis. No matter how much staff a fundraiser has, no matter how much assistance he receives, it is impossible to escape the agonizing and persistent details of the job.

What must concern you is that you not confuse the sheer busyness of working on details with a sense of accomplishment. Attention to details transforms a good program into a great one. An effective fundraiser is a disciple of what is called the "yellow-legal-pad school." Work. Work. Work. Details. Details. Details.

But there are exceptions.

"Details are distracting," Father Hesburgh told me. "I don't believe you can think great thoughts if you are worrying about details. I am convinced that's true. I also don't believe that two people should worry about the same thing. I don't really worry. I let others do that. I'm a good delegator."

Some in the field worry about small things, and they spend all of their time working on them. The small things, the minutia, the picking of nits. What I refer to as details are different—they are the wondrous bits and pieces, the myriad of elements and facets, that convert a prospect into a mega giver. That means being careful to avoid getting so totally wrapped up in the minutia that you never get around to going for the gift. It's easy to get up to your kazoo in minutia, like walking through mud, but the great fundraisers eschew that.

Michaelangelo said that trifles make perfection. And perfection is no trifle. Most of the leaders in my sample are gripped
by what can best be described as a "perfection imperative." They
are driven by it. Mind you, and this is the critical distinction, this
does not mean inattention to little things. It means riveting care
for the small details that make big gifts.

Max Beerbohm said: "How many charming and unfulfilled
talents have been spoiled by the desire to do important work, but
with inattention to details? That determines the difference
between people. Some are born to lift heavy weights. Some are
born to juggle golden balls."

It would be easy to accuse some of the great fundraisers of
spending too much time on details. Some are neurotic on the
subject? I find it very much like the department store magnate,
John Wanamaker who said: "Half the money I spend on advertising is wasted. The trouble is I don't know which half." And
that's the rub: Which half of the time you spend on detail is
wasted?

All of the inspired fundraisers are much the same. There is
nothing quite like the thrill of working on a prospect, developing
precisely the right strategy, determining an imaginative twist,
and uncovering a piece of research that unlocks the whole puzzle.
It's nothing short of discovering the startling beauty and clarity
of a glorious old master painting which had laid buried under
dirt and varnish. Details. That would not come very high on
anyone's love list, but for most of the great ones, the juice is
worth the squeeze.

These men and women, they feel keenly about everything
that relates to their work. Their goals are dreams, visions with
deadlines. For them, progress results from a healthy discontent.
They are almost never satisfied. They seem to be in a perpetual
state of standing on tiptoes, waiting to be kissed.

They are not technicians. Technique has to do with knowing the facts and the mechanics of the job. That's the science of

fundraising. That is helpful. But it has little to do with real greatness.

To be the best in this field, to really excel, what is essential is to understand why people are motivated to action. Why they are willing to be committed to a cause, impelled to give. Having the "know-how" is not important. What really counts is the never-ending exploration and revelation of the "know-why." That is the art.

The exceptional fundraisers have drive, "fire in the belly"— a term you don't hear much these days. They love to win and they love the battle.

The truth is that every person in fundraising is a survivor. He is a survivor or nothing. Winning is everything. That is an overstatement for effect, but very near the mark. There is no happy-ever-aftering for a fundraiser. No matter what the ability, tomorrow is another race. Another test. Another hurdle.

You have got to run faster and faster. And work harder and harder. George Engdahl told me how he was a teacher and a coach and that he understands what it means to work hard. "I think you inspire others—volunteers and staff—by your own work ethic. I work late and I work hard. If I have had any success, it is because I work harder than most people. And I am a winner. I can't stand to lose. I want to win. I can taste it. I never go on a call that I don't want to win. And that's how I deal with my work."

Father Hesburgh told me he had long been fascinated by what makes a champion—the true champion, the legends, the one in a thousand who consistently dominates his opponent, performs at the highest level, at the most crucial time. What makes them different from the near-greats and the also-rans? Skills and supreme confidence in these skills are a part of it, but they are not the dominating factors. "Over the years, I have observed three characteristics which are common in every superstar I have ever known. They are just as applicable in fundraising as they are in the athletic arena. The first is the champion's profound sense of dissatisfaction with his own accomplishments. The second is an ability to peak performance, to get 'up' to a major tournament and event—or major gift. And finally, it's the killer instinct."

My inspired fundraisers are not poor sportsmen—but most of them are hard losers. They follow the dictum: Show me a good loser, and I'll show you a loser. General George S. Patton, in his own special way, said it all: "I wouldn't give a hoot in hell for a man who lost and laughed."

The will to win is the fiber and sinew of all the fundraisers I interviewed. They wouldn't go out to hurt anyone purposely but they do tend to subscribe to the Bronco Nagurski Doctrine. Nagurski was a hurdling, maiming fullback for the old Chicago Bears. He once said: "I wouldn't ever set out to hurt anybody, not deliberately or intentionally—unless it was, you know, something kind of important, like some sort of a football game or something like that."

The successful fundraiser must do and dare, strive and succeed, wage war and win. And, ultimately, you must move your institution to greater heights, and goal-shattering victories.

The former professional football coach George Allen used to tell his players: "Winning is living. Every time you win, you are reborn. Every time you lose, you die a little."

The fundraiser works everyday, as the Spanish say, between a sword and the wall. If by chance you somehow lose the big gift, it is admirable to go down fighting. Ah, but it is far better to win the gift and come out on top.

Listen to what Father Hesburgh told me: " I don't like to lose. I hate to lose. But I also recognize that life is full of defeats and I don't get terribly disturbed if I don't keep winning all the time. But I would have to say that I certainly have more victories than I do defeats. I'm not sure that I would want to be surrounded by good losers. By that, I mean people who don't mind losing. I would think that there is something wrong with a person who doesn't mind losing." My great fundraisers, they mind terribly!

And they are staunch believers in the possible. To them, anything can be accomplished. Miracles happen every day. They also understand that if all possible objections must first be overcome, nothing will ever be accomplished.

Warren Avis feels that ignorance is wonderfully bliss. Like the great fundraisers, he feels that if you know all the pitfalls, you might stumble or never even get started. "To become great, a person must learn that nothing is impossible. I've often said that if I had known how many headaches I was going to face in starting the Avis Rent-A-Car Company, I never would have had the guts to start." But he didn't know all the problems and he didn't know what he couldn't do. And he was so dumb, he just went ahead and did them! When Alice told the Queen: "It is impossible to believe impossible things," the Queen replied: "Fiddlesticks, I've believed as many as six impossible things before breakfast." That's it. That's the operating philosophy of the great fundraiser. The blind faith in the possible.

Fundraisers must have focus. There isn't enough time to do the job properly, to get everything accomplished, to finish every job—this really bothers the group I interviewed. George Engdahl said: "What concerns me most is that I always feel pressed. I don't feel there is enough time to do everything I want to do. I feel, for instance, that I am a very creative person. But I somehow don't seem to have the time to sit back, put my feet up on the desk, and just think. There is too much to do." Vartan Gregorian said: "There simply isn't time. I work 14 to 16 hours a day, but I am always running. There isn't time to reflect. I think that is why I verbalize so much." For a lot of us in the business, talking is easier than reflecting.

George Engdahl is a graduate of California Lutheran College, at the time a school of 1,000 students. There it is again, the small college background. He was highly involved in his church as a young man and thought seriously of going into the ministry. He feels that the strongest people he knows in the field have a deep association and background in the church. George has done it all—fundraising in higher education, the health care field, and with the Chicago Symphony. His symphony raises more money than any in the world, and probably more money than any other organization or institution in Chicago.

And George, he has focus! His drive, compulsion, and every thought is on getting the gift. He loves the adventure and feels it is his strongest suit. "I really love raising funds, I love calling on people. Finding the time to work with my staff is a real concern, but I know it's something I must do. The fact that you don't like to do it has nothing to do with the job—you simply have to get it done." You may have a lot of people in the office doing very important things—the research, the clerical assistance, the writing, all of the things that add to a strong development office. But for those of us out in the field, I feel that our job is to get the gift. Nothing takes the place of that. Everything that goes on in the office should result in getting the gift."

There is a tendency these days in our profession to use euphemisms. It's been polished to an art. It's called marketing, investing, development, advancement—almost anything but fundraising. But fundraising is a high calling. And fundraising is really what it's all about. It's a ministry. John R. Mott said: "Blessed are the fundraisers for in Heaven they shall stand on the right hand of the martyrs."

"It's fundraising," George Engdahl said to me. "I feel that it is the highest and toughest type of selling. It is an exhilarating experience to be able to sell a project. It is the pinnacle. Perhaps the word 'selling' is not quite the proper term—I know today people in our business talk about 'investing' but you really are selling a concept, a belief in the future."

Fundraising is motivating and asking others to share with you in a great adventure, a vision, a dream. It is inciting others to feel the magic, the drama of the program. It is bringing to your enterprise a zealous combination of energy, enthusiasm, and sheer talent.

Some in the business have lost "the fire in the belly." It takes a daring-do attitude. Some are too cautious, careful, obedient. Thin tie, thin skin. The right working conditions, the right employment contract, the right suburb, the right car, the right boat. The great ones I interviewed strive for perfection. They're non-stop machines. Every task is filled with the substance of their dreams—getting the gift.

Some institutions have what I call "organization encrustration." They are rigid. Frozen in time. They will not move, they will not act. They are covered with the five barnacles that will finally sink them: It won't work here, we've tried it before, it's not in the budget, it's not the right time, and we've never done that sort of thing before.

I say caution to the winds! We need to encourage our institutions and boards to create an environment that inspires us to attempt new ideas, plan new dreams, create new visions.

A promising junior executive at IBM was involved in a risky venture for the company and managed to lose over ten million dollars in the undertaking. Thomas Watson, IBM's founder and inspiration, called the young man into his office. For good reason, the junior executive was nervous. "I imagine you want my resignation." Watson said: "You can't be serious. We've just spent ten million dollars educating you." We shall never fulfill our boldest dreams unless we are given the succor to succeed.

But don't make the same mistake twice! I know one person in our business who sunk an enormous amount of money into buying the mailing list of an up-scale magazine—extremely high flying, high income subscribers. An expensive package was designed and developed. As close as the management can figure, not counting overhead and staff time, it spent $60,000 on the mailing. The return produced $120. No one was pleased! But okay, it was an educated guess. Hindsight is always keener, but in retrospect, it seemed worth the try. A year later, she bought the same mailing list and used essentially the same package. With the same results. She was given her severance!

I find that the opportunity is actually there, there for the taking. The board is willing, just waiting for the right inspiration. Too many in the field, however, are reluctant to move—anesthetized with the fear of making a mistake. They will analyze, survey, research, evaluate, assess—into a state of "analysis paralysis." What they won't do is raise funds.

Richard F. Wilson, president of the NSFRE, told me of something that happened to him when he first started in the business in Milwaukee. He was with the Boy Scouts. At that time, only a few were involved in Planned Giving. It wasn't called that then—he was helping people write their wills.

Only three or four men in Milwaukee were really working at this then, and they would get together on a monthly basis to talk about their work and progress. They had been meeting for months and Dick Wilson was becoming discouraged. At each meeting, someone would bring a copy of a magnificent new folder, four colors, and many folds. Another would talk about a sophisticated system he was using for identifying prospects—at that time, sticking a long needle through cards punched with holes. It was the manual forerunner of the computer. Another talked about research.

After months of listening to all of this, Dick finally confessed to the group his great distress. He didn't have the fancy system or the slick folders. He finally asked them, "Fellas, how much have you been raising?" To his absolute surprise, none had yet gotten around to asking for a gift. They had been taking all this time getting ready. Analysis paralysis! Dick didn't know he was supposed to be doing all of this preparation work. He just went out and started calling on people . . . and with great success, writing wills and getting gifts.

Napoleon sat through two hours of a magnificent full-dress review of one of his General's command. The precision was a marvel to behold. The display, the marching, the intricate demonstration of arms —it was breathtaking. Napoleon turned to his General and said: "This is glorious . . . but it is not war." Too many in our field prepare gloriously, but never wage war.

The great fundraisers believe in the concept of: Ready. Fire. Aim. They believe that doing something, even if it's not precisely right, is better than doing nothing at all.

Ross Perot talks about the difference between Electronic Data Systems and General Motors: "The first EDS-er to see a snake, kills it. At GM, the first thing that you do is organize a committee on snakes. Then you bring in a consultant who knows a lot about snakes. The third thing you do is talk about it for a year." What Perot didn't mention is that you probably have a meeting to appoint a committee to study the question! "If you don't have the stomach to develop a plan, to develop a strategy, to take the hits and win the fight—I say you're just a kind of morning glory. You're gonna wilt by noon."

At what point do you simply stop? Relax? Work less hard, less intensively, less compulsively? When do you stop trying to climb the highest mountains? Never. At least not the great fundraisers. In this business, you either grow or go. A healthy impatience and dogged persistence was common in all those I interviewed.

No matter how great the fundraiser, rejections occur. Some prospects will not accept your proposal. Being rejected is not something you invented. It happens to us all. In this business, it is simply taken as a given that somewhere along the line, you are going to be turned down. It goes with the territory. Just don't lose more often than you win!

Keep in mind, when a prospect turns you down, you haven't failed. You've just been given a new opportunity. You made the wrong proposal. Or you didn't do your research properly. Or you've been courting the wrong prospect. Remember what Schuller said—there are no bad fundraisers, only bad dreams. Keep on trying. Keep on working. Be a pupil of Longfellow who learns "to labor and to wait." But labor!

Frank Washburn is the untiring and determined YMCA Director who raised millions for Blue Ridge Assembly in North Carolina. Scotty, as he is known by all, is tenacity exemplified. To him, "no" does not mean "never." "If you go out on a call and you are not successful—go back, and go back, and go back again. Keep going back until you are successful."

One of the members of this board said: "If it's doable and Scotty makes up his mind he wants to do it, you can be certain it will be done." Washburn says: "I never stop. I just keep going back. I've had people tell me they weren't going to give and I nod my head and I keep going back and I keep asking. And sooner or later, they give."

Persistence pays off. It is the one factor that is certain to lead to success. Our greatest glory is not in never failing, but in rising every time we fall.

Dr. William Menninger, founder of the famed Menninger Clinic, ought to know. He says that some people "work along in a hum-drum way, interested only in their salary check. They don't have a goal. When anyone crosses them, they take their marbles and walk out. The people who go places and do things make the most of every situation. They are ready for the next thing that comes along on the road to their goal. They know what they want and are willing to go an extra mile. They persist."

They do not give up, these high achievers I interviewed. There are disappointments and valleys. At times, deep valleys. But they meet this head-on.

Home run hitters strike out, politicians suffer defeat, and even the best songwriters produce songs that no one sings. The great fundraisers understand this. But somehow, they reach deep down for some inner strength.

I suspect you won't be surprised that I find many of the great fundraisers are often stubborn. They don't refuse advice —but they don't accept it easily! They thrive on people, but they go it alone. They understand "the art of compromise," but at the very minimum they are satisfied with nothing less than what Lyndon Johnson used to refer to as "areas of attainability"—the thesis that it is better to secure part of a goal rather than to lose the whole.

The inspired ones believe in moving forward, taking the action, the bold step. They live by the dictum that it's easier to ask for forgiveness than it is to get permission. "It may be a failing," says Boone Powell, "but when something requires my taking bold, immediate action, I don't always have time to get board action." There is a wise, old Hebrew saying that if you really want to eat it, don't ask if it's kosher!

Persistence pays off. I could give you hundreds of examples. Here's a recent one.

Alfred Ball was a good friend of Scripps Memorial Hospitals and had been a regular donor for years. One day, he had an emergency and was taken to the Trauma Center at Scripps for immediate treatment. No one knows for certain what happened, but evidently it was a horrible experience. Everything that could go wrong did. He was beside himself. He was enraged. (Why is it that sort of thing always seems to happen to our best friends and largest donors? It's Murphy's Law in spades: If something can go wrong, it will!)

Mr. Ball's attorney called Jim Bowers the next day and told him that Mr. Ball would never give to the hospital again and further more, he was taking the institution out of his will. Now that will get your attention!

That was several years ago. What did Jim Bowers do? Well for one thing, he never gave up. He started by writing the proper note of apology. He continued to keep Ball on the mailing list—even though the attorney said that Ball had requested that his name be deleted. Jim continued to send him birthday greetings each year. A poinsettia plant every Christmas. Invitations to special events and dinners. The effective hospital newsletter continued to go to Ball's home on a regular basis. Jim continued to call him and to write letters. He never gave up.

Several months ago, after a lapse of three years, Ball again made a gift for annual support. When he died shortly after that, he left an estate of $4 million—three-quarters of which he directed to be given to Scripps Memorial Hospitals.

Everyone who knows Mr. Ball is certain that this would not have happened without the persistence of Jim Bowers. More than $3 million to Scripps Memorial Hospitals because Jim Bowers never gave up.

"Never give in. Never give in! Never, never, never, never—in nothing great or small, large or petty—never give in. . . ." Winston Churchill said that. He understood the philosophy of winning.

It's easy to find oyster shells. It takes extraordinary perseverance to find the pearl. An invincible determination can accomplish almost anything. Strong will, a focused purpose, these qualities mixed generously with determination—that marks the distinction between good fundraisers and the great ones.

Francis Cardinal Spellman was from New York, likely the greatest Roman Catholic fundraiser of this century. Note well his tenacity!

Cardinal Spellman heard that an eccentric, wealthy Protestant woman had in her old age become greatly enamored with the Catholic church. He lost no time in gaining an introduction and a visit. She was Mabel Corey, a former chorus girl, and the widow of the former president of U.S. Steel. It was her storybook leap to great fortune that immortalized her in song: "She's Only a Bird in a Gilded Cage." She wasn't too pleased with that!

The Cardinal courted her, and Mrs. Corey swiftly learned the joys of being one of his very favorite friends. She enjoyed personal tours of the cathedral and special lunches and teas. He sent her holy pictures and a crucifix. And regular notes. He never missed an opportunity.

Once, she expressed a bizarre desire to live in a convent. He lost no time. He spent the better part of a night badgering Mother Superiors of convents in his diocese. He finally found one. And again, he never missed an opportunity. He persisted. He would often visit her on the way home from a banquet, often grabbing a dessert and flowers from the head table, as a present for her. When Mrs. Corey took brief holidays, Spellman made the chancellery priest turn out to wave goodbye at the train station. She delighted in all of the fuss.

Cardinal Spellman was rewarded when she died—Mrs.

Dorey entrusted him with $15 million for the work of the church.

An old Scottish ballad goes: "I'm hurt but I'm not slain. I lie me down and rest a bit, and then I'll fight again."

I have searched for the author and while I have seen it many times, I can't discover who deserved the credit for this magnificent statement: Nothing in the world can take the place of persistence. Talent will not. Nothing is more common than unsuccessful men of talent. Genius will not. The world is full of educated derelicts. Persistence and determination alone are omnipotent.

The dictum "Press on" has solved and always will answer the problems of the human race. Harriet Beecher Stowe said that when you get into a tight place and everything seems to be going against you, and you feel you cannot hold on for a minute longer, "Never give up, for that is just the place in time that the tide will turn."

Never give in. Never! Everything is difficult before it becomes easy. Go after your objective with all of the vigor and fervor possible, as if there was nothing else in the world that mattered for the moment. Brian Lurie says: "You have to have dogged determination—year in and year out. You have to operate on your own power. There has to be an inner-drive. And a tremendous amount of energy that keeps you going."

A magnificent saying goes: "The situation is totally hopeless . . . but not serious!" To the great fundraiser, nothing is serious. All things are possible. They understand that all things can be accomplished with the proper drive and determination. Serious? Never.

Boone Powell, Sr. taught me a magnificent lesson. He told me the story of one of the major gifts he received that had been nurtured over a long period. "My philosophy is that when we receive a gift, that should be only the beginning. I remember one person in particular, a really lovely man, who started making small gifts to Baylor Medical Center. I'd take him to meetings, send him notes, and do whatever I could to remind him about the hospital. I just kept working on him.

"At first, he wasn't really interested in giving but I kept working at it. It took a lot of time but in the end, he gave us $17 million. There's another fellow, and I must say that he was really a hard nut to crack. I called on him and called on him for years—but with no success. When he finally made the gift, he was so happy that he couldn't thank me enough. He just couldn't thank me enough!

"It taught me a lesson. You can't give up. You can never give up. This man started with a fairly small gift but he ended up making a very large one.

"I remember another one just like that—from a man who had given us a $100,000 for a major piece of therapy equipment. But I've always figured that the first gift shouldn't be the largest. As a matter of fact, it's almost always the smallest. With the right kind of care and attention, it should grow. This fellow ended up giving millions to us. We just kept after him. I remember him telling me once: 'I've never done anything I've enjoyed more in my life than giving a gift to Baylor Medical Center'." Persistence paid off for everyone.

Admiral Hyman Rickover says: "Nothing worthwhile can be accomplished without determination. In the early days of nuclear power, getting approval to build the first nuclear submarine—the *Nautilus*—was accepted as being as difficult as designing and building it. Good ideas are not adopted automatically. They must be driven into practice with courageous patience and persistence.

Milton Murray is like a gentle bulldog—it may appear that his tail is wagging, but he never lets go! "Perseverance is extremely important to me. You've got to keep at things. Keep working at them. You have to keep at it until the very moment of truth. I think the thing that helps me the most is that I'm a self-starter. I have lots of perseverance. Some people can be enthusiastic about their work for a few months, some for a year or so. I've been enthusiastic about my work for 30 years, and I think it's paid off. I never quit."

Both Father Hesburgh and Buck Smith agree that the quality can be learned and nurtured. "You are not born with a drive to keep on going," Hesburgh told me. "It is something you achieve, step by step, day by day. With the right attitude, it grows and matures." Buck Smith concurs: "I doubt you're born with the attribute of perseverance, but you learn it at an early age. It's something that becomes part of a person. And I find that you are either the type of person who perseveres, or you are not. And if you do not persevere, you are a loser."

Louis Pasteur said that the great secret and strength which led him each time to his objective rested solely in his tenacity. John Miltner told me that our business is filled with ups and downs. "From the standpoint of fundraising, there are as many times that you are down as there are when you are up. It keeps going on. 'No' doesn't really mean 'no.' You've got to keep going back. To be successful in our field requires perseverance."

The surest way to guarantee success is to plan for it. Let me give you a general summation of what my great fundraisers told me. First of all—and for some it was the most important factor—these fundraisers were convinced that whatever the objective, it could be accomplished. They believe in it so strongly, they can feel it and touch it. Many of them then set a date that is aggressively optimistic—one that makes them reach for the stars. But they know that they can do it and they set their mind on "can do."

They become consumed with achieving their objective. Getting the gift, winning the campaign—that becomes their unrelenting dedication. Nothing gets in the way.

And then, they talk about it. Yes! They let everyone in the world know what their goal is. They find that it helps put them on the spot. But more than that, it actually makes the goal seem more attainable—mentally and emotionally.

And last, they never give up. Not ever. They pursue their objective, not matter what the obstacles. They pursue, persist, persevere. And they win.

Life is action. Fundraising is a combination of visions, plans, and action. Father Hesburgh told me: "I'm an action person. I tend to move on things. I can't imagine having a great dream or developing an important program without taking the next necessary step, which is to put the dream into action. And I think that important men and women like to be around action people. An action-oriented person tends to motivate action on the part of others." Boone Powell, Sr. has been responsible for millions of dollars of bequests for his beloved Baylor University Medical Center. But he's impatient and thrives on action. "I was never very keen on waiting for a bequest. I'd want to get the gift while the person was still alive. That's how you can make them really happy."

Action—John Miltner says that may perhaps be the most significant factor. "In my judgment, being action-oriented is one of the most important factors in being a good fundraiser. You have to be driven. You have to move. And this becomes complicated because there are so many distractions. There's one meeting after another. Research. Carrying through. You have to keep at it all the time and this takes a great deal of discipline."

The staff meetings, the executive cabinet sessions, and the marketing and research numbers—they'll statistic the creative fundraiser to death. The inspired ones aren't often very good about attending conferences and seminars, not unless they are leading them. They are the doers. They study, practice, apply, and implement. Their shelves are almost certainly lined with self-improvement books, and they listen to "how to" cassettes when they drive their cars. They don't lose a minute. They'll do almost anything to get up to speed. They think and work harder, longer, and better than their competitors.

****

7   Making Great Things Happen

Pheidippids is famed for his 26 mile run from the plains of Marathon to Athens. It was a monumental achievement. Arriving in Athens, he gasps, "Rejoice, we conquer." But remember, he died!

"They told me to cheer up, things could be worse. So I cheered up and, sure enough . . . things got worse!"

A fundraiser I heard about had fallen ill and had to miss one of the meetings of the board. At his hospital bedside, he received a copy of a resolution by the board of directors, wishing him a speedy return to work—on which the corporate secretary had dutifully recorded "approved by a vote six to four."

As I said earlier, fundraisers are survivors. They cannot be compared to a target in an ordinary shooting gallery. The target in a gallery has a chance of not getting hit! But for the fundraiser, escape is impossible. Your shooting gallery is shaped like a merry-go-round. And you are in the center. The bullets come from all sides and at all times. If you raise your revenue, you have a chance at the gold ring. At least for another year.

It's exhausting work. And exhilarating. A glorious pressure-cooker. That is why a healthy sense of humor is needed. No one rates a sense of humor higher than Jim Bowers. It is one of the major factors he looks for when he selects new staff. "Fundraising is a series of disappointments sprinkled with an occasional surprise. Without a sense of humor, those disappointments could really get you down."

It's a tough business, interspersed with some mountain top experiences. But most of the time, it's just plain tough. There's the story about the university president who died and went to hell. His students were not surprised. His faculty had predicted it, and his trustees had arranged it. Worst of all, he was there a whole term before he realized he was not on campus!

Father Hesburgh told me he thought he had an excellent sense of humor. "I try not to take myself too seriously. I know that you can't do everything by yourself. The important thing is to surround yourself with good people. But I consider a sense of humor to be essential." Carl Lindner is the chairman of the American Financial Corporation. He says: "My secret for success is a sense of humor, persistence, and imagination. And I put them in that order." All of the great fundraisers I interviewed exhibited a keen sense of humor and none took himself too seriously.

No one can think clearly when his fists are clenched and his heart is heavy. A sense of humor reduces people and their problems to their proper proportion.

And it takes luck, too. Good fortune may be what some call "just plain luck." But more often, it is the result of ability and instinct, mixed thoroughly with knowledge. And being at the right place at the right time.

Sometimes it appears something very special has happened and it occurred "by accident." But some argue that nothing ever happens by accident, that everything that happens in our lives occurs because we will it to happen.

"The lucky" fundraisers make things happen. Their good fortune is a result of something that is created, directed, influenced, and made to happen. Good fortune and luck play a significant role in winning. This assumes that the fundraiser is capable and knows an opportunity when he sees one. The successful fundraiser is one who sees the chance, and takes it. Good fortune and luck should be cultivated.

The harder you work, the luckier you get.

Luck means the hardships and agonies you do not hesitate to endure. The long nights you devote to work, writing a case statement, preparing a grant proposal, designing a strategy. Luck means the appointments you never fail to keep, the planes you never fail to catch. Opportunity only knocks once, they say. But some never hear it knocking at all.

Jeffrey Blum provides some interesting guides for an article he wrote in *Redbook* magazine, "How To Get Lucky." He says that first of all, and probably most important, you have to work very hard to get lucky. You must think and concentrate on good luck. Then, he says, you have to void all negative thought patterns. Instead, create positive and optimistic thoughts. He says you should experiment, take risks with new opportunities. Take a chance. Some fail to take full advantage of the many opportunities presented. But the world has not failed in offering them.

Luck can be made to happen. As Louis Pasteur said: "Luck favors the prepared mind." Gary Player, the great golfer, said that the more he practiced, the luckier he got.

There is a difference between "chance" and "luck." Some think they mean the same, but they don't. Chance might be best described as an infinite number of unpredictable happenings, each of which can be an opportunity. These opportunities must be seized. Each of us in this fundraising business is surrounded by these opportunities, these chances. Acting on them, pouncing on them, brings about luck. We are all surrounded by chance. It is up to us to turn these opportunities into lucky breaks.

Louis Nizer is one of the nation's most highly esteemed trial attorneys. He was once asked if there was such a thing as luck in trial law. "Yes, but it only comes in the library at three o'clock in the morning while I'm doing my research." Well into his eighties, he says that still holds true for him. And you will still find him in the library at three o'clock in the morning, seeking luck! When you stop working, the lucky coincidences stop happening.

"Fortune favors the bold." This is an old Latin aphorism —and it seems to be substantiated in an unusual way. Max Gunther is considered to be an expert in the luck phenomena. He says that as a group, lucky people tend to be bold people. "The most timid men and women I have met in my travels have also been, with some exceptions, the least lucky." Boldness helps create good luck.

Luck is not always something you can mention in the presence of a self-made man. But most of my great fundraisers talked about their really good fortune. Vartan Gregorian told me: "I've been one of the luckiest people alive. Everything that has happened to me has been by sheer luck and happenstance. I work hard, I have above average intelligence, and I believe I understand people. But timing has controlled my life. All of the wonderful things that have happened to me have been the result of good fortune. I work terribly hard, and yes, I think a person makes his own luck. Luck has been part of the excitement of my life. I have always been ready to seize the opportunity and to assume the challenge."

Those who really wish to grow in our profession work hard to improve their abilities and perfect their skills. But I find very few who make a conscientious effort to improve their luck. There is strong evidence that this can be done. Just like those "acres of diamonds" in our own backyard, most people don't recognize all of the opportunities and possibilities around them. There is emphatic belief that luck is similar to intelligence. It can be increased with the proper exercise. Everyone has the potential.

I commend you to the "four laws of luck." Make a commitment to working at them, believing in them. I promise you, it will make a difference.

1) Be audacious. I have already pointed out that luck favors those who are bold. Louisa May Alcott said: "Resolve to take fate by the throat and shake a living out of her." At times it takes extraordinary courage to reach out and grab hold of an opportunity, but boldness begets luck. You have to be willing to take the chance.

2) Someone said that at the very most, we are only seven people away from meeting a person that we want to contact. Today, that's called networking. It means that if you want to call on a top prospect, it is almost certain that you know someone who has a friend, who has a brother-in-law, who golfs with a person, who went to school . . . and so the network goes. You

can become lucky through networking. And that's the trick for the effective fundraiser. It means putting yourself in key places where you are almost certain to meet new people.

3) Have faith in your intuition. Hunches pay off. Some say intuition is like a computer—a backlog of information stored in the mind. It slushes around in the subconscious. And just when you need it most, this mind-computer is able to give you a "mental printout" of all the information you need. You didn't realize it was there, but it is. Those times when you think "I don't know why this seems like the right decision, it just feels right," that's your mental computer working for you.

4) You have to think lucky. Work at it. Recognize those great opportunities when they strike. See them as something that happens to you. When you count on having good luck, you get it. Your attitude means everything.

The successful fundraiser is the one who had the chance and grabbed it!

The Jewish community in San Francisco is now a power to be reckoned with in international Jewish life. Almost everyone credits this transformation to Rabbi Brian Lurie, director of the Jewish Welfare Federation. The federation in San Francisco now ranks third nationally in per capita giving—behind only long-time powerhouses in Cleveland and Detroit.

Before Rabbi Lurie arrived, San Francisco ranked far down the list. Under his leadership, its income has tripled to the $18 million it raises each year. Its endowment has grown from $6 million to $30 million.

The Jewish Community was once known as "closed"—run by old-time San Francisco families. Lurie opened it up! Under his leadership—rated as nothing less than dynamic—the federation finds itself at the forefront of a national trend to offer more support to Jewish education and to orthodox institutions. According to a recent newspaper article: ". . . Lurie looks like a Hollywood star, talks like a deep-thinking, emphatic Guru, and acts like a dynamic corporate executive. He is touted as a 'world class Jewish leader' and part of the international Jewish conspiracy." Around the country, they speak of his charisma as well as his efficiency. One of his peers says: "He's incredibly effective. A superstar."

What makes Lurie great? I have met many in this business who I felt really did not enjoy raising money. That shouldn't be too shocking. Many dentists, for instance, probably don't love their work. Many in the ministry realize it was not truly their calling. This surely is the case in every profession. In fundraising, many men and women enjoy writing case statements, doing research, or working with computers. But they will never be the great ones.

The giants in this field lust for raising money. Brian Lurie is one: "It happens that I love raising money. For me, the thrill never ends. But I would not do fundraising for the sake of raising money. Not if I didn't believe in the cause. I really believe in what I am doing." Lurie believes emphatically in the importance of the cause. That makes the difference. He says qualities are essential in the business. You have to love people, you have to be a good communicator, and you have to be a superb listener. But most of all you must have a commitment to your cause.

Terry Sanford was president of Duke University from 1969 through 1984. He said that he had no quarrel with someone who moved from university to university, but chances are that he would not hire such a person. He said that he felt long tenure in an institution was a key element and more than that—and here's the important point—the person should be someone who loves Duke University passionately.

Passion for your cause and for your institution propels you to success. Passion and commitment, a marriage of a dedicated soul on fire in a great cause. William Hutchison Murray says that the moment one definitely commits himself to a great cause, providence moves, too. All sorts of things occur to help one that would never otherwise have happened. A flowing stream of events issues from the decision, raising in one's favor all manner of unforeseen happy occurrences and material assistance—which no one could have dreamt would have come their way.

One of Bruce Heilman's colleagues told me that when he met with the faculty for the first time at the University of Richmond, he said to them: "With your help, I'm going to make this a great university. I am totally dedicated to that cause. I am going to be spending just about all of my time raising funds. I am committed to that. This means that I may not be on the campus every time you need me. It means that you are going to have to go to someone else with your problems because I'll be out raising funds to make this a great university. I'm committed to that."

Joel P. Smith is adamant that we must have respect and a commitment for our institutions—their origin, history, character, and vision for the future. "We must understand why we do what we do, and if we are different, why we are different. As successful fundraisers, it is imperative that we each have a conviction about the merit, worth, and singularity of the organization that we represent. Donors, in my experience, read this conviction with remarkable acuity." Smith says that effective fundraisers are not fast-talking salespeople trying to bring a quick buck to the institution. They are people who share and convey a deep belief in the merit and worth of the institution they represent.

Heilman told me the story of how, when he first came to the university, Mr. Claude Robbins told him that he wanted to make a large gift to the University of Richmond to make it the greatest small university in the country. This resulted in a $50 million gift. Since then, the family has given over $100 million. But he said, he made the Robbins' commitment his own—to make it the greatest small university in the country. It was this belief in the cause that makes the difference. "I am totally, completely wound up in my work. I think that's why some are especially good in this business. They become totally dedicated to the cause. That makes it a great deal of fun, also."

Father Hesburgh thought back to his early years. "Fundraising is part of my job. You shouldn't have this kind of responsibility in the first place if you don't expect to get out and work at it. If you really believe in your work and you believe in your institution and your mission, raising money is simply something you have to do. And I really believe in what I am doing. I don't consider myself an effective salesman at all. I joined the order to get away from raising money. I didn't like it at all. When I was a young priest, I was in a parish that was badly in debt and I decided then and there I wasn't going to spend my life raising money. I took the vow of poverty. Well here I am! It's not exactly what I had in mind when I started out, but you do what you have to do, and I really believe in this place."

This same characteristic appears in all of the giant fund-raisers. Their sense of mission. Mission is their single driving force. Some say they do not recognize it consciously, but they do have the will and the dedication to excel. And because their work is a mission, they become zealous achievers, able to accomplish objectives others feel are out of reach. Vartan Gregorian said that he didn't take his position at the Library as a job. He took it as a mission. He says that he resolved to bring his whole person into the responsibility and fling the whole weight of his being into it.

Buck Smith said to me: "It takes great commitment and passion to be really good in this field. There are times that you become so focused, the work is your whole life. Everything has to be just right. Perfect. And you can't do that without commitment and passion."

Only when a person feels mightily about the mission of the institution, only if he can work with all his dedication and devotion—only then can he work with great heart and cheerfulness. This commitment to the cause assures all things can be accomplished.

There may not be any mystery to it at all. If you truly believe in your cause, and you do the right things at the right time, and persevere—you are almost assured that you will do well and that you will be successful. A belief and a commitment to the cause, it makes great things happen. It puts the wind to your back. It makes the difference. It transforms an opportunity into a successful venture.

****

8 Running Fast Just to Stand in Place

"There's nothing in a caterpillar that tells you it is going to be a beautiful butterfly. Who knows what any man can become?"
—R. Buckminster Fuller

"In the following pages, I offer nothing more than simple facts, plain arguments, and common sense; and have no other preliminaries to settle with the reader, other than that he will divest himself of prejudice and prepossessions, and suffer his reason and his feelings to determine for themselves . . ."
—Thomas Paine

In Texas, they tell the story about three men having dinner at Dallas' Petroleum Club.

"I figure I've got about 200,000 acres in the Panhandle, maybe more," says one fellow over coffee. "And, I've got two more ranches about that size across the state. I guess I've got about a million head of cattle all together."

"I've got about the same number of acres," says the second. "I can't remember where all my fields are, but they're mostly in oil."

The third, W.A. Criswell, says: "You guys sure have me beat. I only have six blocks—all in downtown Dallas, of course!"

I don't think Dr. Criswell would really appreciate the story, but the person who told it to me has infinite esteem and affection for Criswell. I found that just about everyone does.

Dr. W.A. Criswell is senior pastor of the First Baptist Church in Dallas. It is the largest Baptist Church in the country. He has nearly 27,000 members, and an additional 5,000 children too young for baptism. Billy Graham has been a member of the church for 34 years and considers it his "home church."

Criswell was born in El Dorado, Oklahoma, a city of 600 people. When he went to Baylor University, it had 900 students. He is an effervescent 78 year old, sparkling eyes, joyous and righteous in spirit, dignified but totally without pomp. He somehow reminds me of a Doberman pinscher that has been to finishing school. He is disciplined and quite proper—but you'd better do what he says!

Emerson said that an institution is the length and shadow of one man. There is no better example than Criswell and his church. He is single of purpose, narrow of focus, and is undergirded by a burning dedication to his church. How does he raise his funds? "By prayer, love, and labor."

His mind never stops. He prides himself on doing more and more, leading more vigorously, creating dreams and more dreams. For two years, he served as president of the Southern Baptist Convention. The convention represents the largest denomination in this country and in that group, even among those who do not agree with Criswell on every count, there is no question about the respect he is accorded. He is regarded as one of the greatest leaders in the denomination. At First Baptist, there is nothing less than total devotion and reverence for the man.

We talked in his office. He sat on the very edge of his chair. "I don't preach because it is that special time on Sunday. The Word must burn like a fire in my bones."

In the last ten years, he has raised $50 million in capital funds and about $100 million in annual support. The budget of the First Baptist is the largest of any church in the country—not another is even one-third the size. The six square blocks in downtown Dallas I referred to is not too much of a stretch. There is the huge church, with all of the additions. A very large parking structure. A large seminary which Criswell has built.

I heard another story about Criswell, and I suspect he wouldn't appreciate this one either! Someone told me that he went to Heaven. They had trouble finding his name under "Minister." Then they tried the B's for "Baptist." They still couldn't find it. Then they tried the S's for "Scholar." St. Peter simply couldn't find his name anywhere until someone suggested they look under: Real Estate! Few churches in this nation occupy land as valuable as the First Baptist in Dallas.

His workload is of elephantine proportions, but he does not consider himself a workaholic. He told me that he has finally decided that he has to slow down a bit. It is getting more difficult for him to take those out of town speaking dates each week. After all, he is 78. He has cut down to twelve hours a day. Of course, he still performs marriages every Saturday of the year, and preaches three sermons every Sunday. Criswell told me that he really doesn't consider himself a fundraiser. "I don't really ask for gifts. But I do know how to strongly encourage them!"

I was truly impressed. He is a powerful presence that totally dominates and fills the room. A very strong face and a warm, inviting personality. You cannot be with him without feeling that you are in the presence of a Godly man.

In the course of our discussion, I raised the question about his possible retirement. I discovered it was not the kind of topic you discuss with Criswell! "Retirement? Why should I retire? I'm not working. You can't call this work. When you can get up seven days a week and do what you do and what you enjoy doing, that's not work. These 12 or 14 hours a day I have at the Church, I'm not working—I'm having magnificent fun. It's not work. It's just plain fun."

The men and women who really succeed in our profession are the select few who have the ambition and the will. A dedication to their cause. And the burning drive and single-mindedness that propels them to success. In the case of Criswell, there is shirt-sleeved eloquence combined with action. In his presence I was convinced that he could take a button and make a suit out of it!

What impressed me most about Criswell was his highly charged energy. You felt surrounded by it. Like being in the eye of a tornado. And I found this same quality, this inexhaustible energy and drive, to be common in every one of the great fundraisers I interviewed.

These high achievers are indefatigable. From some internal reservoir, they seem to be able to bring forth a torrent capacity to go on doing things. And then to go on and on. For almost unlimited periods of time. Every one of my great fundraisers demonstrated this same capacity. There is evidence in each of the restlessness of the unbridled entrepreneur. They each seem to understand that the speed and energy of the leader determines the pace of the organization.

I found it fascinating that those inspired fundraisers I interviewed all seemed to get along on very few hours of sleep. They weren't particularly proud of the fact, but most of them spoke about it. Bob Schuller told me: "I have a tremendous amount of energy, but everybody runs out of steam once in a while. I don't like to give in or slow down when I'm tired. I'm usually able to just keep on going. Something inside keeps driving me on."

The effective fundraiser must have the energy to initiate and sustain action so that good intentions and dreams are transformed into reality. There is a stressful sense that there is so much to do, and so little time left to do it in. Typical of what I heard was Vartan Gregorian's comment: "I only get three hours of sleep a night—on a good night, four hours. I don't think this is necessarily good, it's just the way I am. I have so much to do and I only have 20 years left to do it in."

Peak performers are filled with intense, concentrated energy. Not nervous energy but the type that exudes enthusiasm and joy.

Jim Bowers told me: "I've always had a very high level of energy. Even when I don't feel up to it, I try to portray a sense of energy. I think it is invigorating and contagious. At times our workload forces us to put in 60 or 70 hours a week. I'm finding that as I get older, I don't have quite the energy I did ten or 20 years ago. That's natural. But I don't think I ever show it. I think people really enjoy being around someone who is highly charged." W.A. Criswell says: "Most of the work of the world is done by people who don't feel well or are too tired to go on. But the ones who succeed are the ones who simply get up and get going, and do what needs to be done.''

Organizations struggle continually for the philanthropic dollar. The competition is only a hot breath behind you, no matter how fast you run. If you stand still, it will swallow you whole.

Bruce Heilman put it right on the line for me—a clear message for all of us in this business: "I used to need only four hours of sleep a night but I find now that I have to get a bit more. I guess that's a sign of age. It is literally true that I start every working day when I am in Richmond with a breakfast meeting. That means I usually get to the office around six or six-thirty in the morning. I usually finish at my desk at home around nine o'clock, cleaning up some of the details of the day and dictating some letters. That doesn't mean that I'm busy every minute. We do a great deal of entertaining and we go out a good bit. That's part of my job. And I do a lot of things in the community and serve on a lot of boards. That's part of my job, too. I have a tremendous amount of energy. I think that to be effective in this work, you have to. If someone doesn't want to maintain that kind of a schedule, they ought to look for a different line of work."

"You can't wait around for people to motivate you," says Boone Powell, Sr., "If you want to succeed, you've got to get up and go. That takes drive and energy. If you don't have it, you'll be left with an empty collection plate."

From where does this well of energy spring? We understand that it is critical to success in our field. This is likely true of any field. John Shad recently gave the Harvard Business School its largest gift ever—$20 million. He says he has observed three common characteristics in outstanding people: Significantly above average motivation, intelligence, and energy. Vauven argues that more fortunes are made by energy than prudence.

Some are born with the capacity to do more and to keep going, hour after hour. But this can be learned also. Most of us work and struggle until we come to the point where we say: "I'll have to stop. I haven't any more energy. I'll drop if I go a moment longer. But the eminent psychologist, William James, said that beyond the barrier of fatigue, a tremendous reservoir of power and energy waits for us. Just waits for us to use if we will just force ourself to use it. "The people who really do great things in this world," said James, "are those who drive past the first layer of fatigue."

Among the great fundraisers I spoke with, a number had been at the business a long time, and were at least beginning to feel their age. But even among this group, they talked to me about needing to work longer and harder, run faster. So when Ulysses speaks, we hear ourselves: "And though we are not now the strength which in old days moved earth and heaven, that which we are, we are—made weak by time and fate, but strong in will to strive, to seek, to find, and not to yield." Not to yield. Enduring, surviving, succeeding in our work, does not stop with age. Indeed, we should grow even more skillful as the years pass. We don't give in. We don't give up. We live and endure. We know better than others the dictum of Tennyson that it is dull to stop, to make an end, to rest unburnished. We shine and add luster by our work and years.

William Beausay is a sports psychologist. He has tested middle linebackers and Indianapolis 500 drivers. He finds them both to be cut from the same cloth. They are nervous, dominant, hostile, aggressive, and impulsive. All are energy-driven and they all peform magnificently. The same can be said for the effective fundraiser. And they are all self-starters.

Father Hesburgh told me: "I can't imagine people being successful in this work, or in any field for that matter, if they aren't self-starters. I wouldn't want to have people around me who weren't able to get up and go at it. I think all the strong people in fundraising have a certain attitude of get up and go."

The effective fundraiser has the vision of success and the energy to make it happen. He moves. He sees the action that is necessary, and he wills it. By his energy and enthusiasm, he empowers others to follow.

Energy is the essential essence of a successful fundraiser in the same sense in which energy is the fundamental concept in physics. But as important as it is, not everyone is endowed with unlimited drive and energy. Thomas Aquinas makes the point that "It is necessary for the perfection of human society there would be men who devote their lives to contemplation and silence." But not the effective fundraiser. Not he. Energy, drive, momentum—these make up the fundraiser's credo.

An impatient lot, these great fundraisers—they don't always wait for consensus or group action. In his best seller, *Success*, Michael Korda writes that "the fastest way to succeed is to look as though you are playing by the rules, but quietly are playing by your own." Some wisdom appears in the theory that nothing is ever accomplished by a committee—unless it consists of three members, one of whom happens to be sick and the other absent. One of my great fundraisers said that if all development committees were laid end-to-end, they would still never reach a conclusion. For the great fundraisers it's on your mark, go. For them, there is no "getting set."

I found that along with this tremendous drive and energy, there is also consuming discipline. To be great at this business, you have to be unrelenting. It requires concentration and diligence. And the willingness to keep at it. Hour after hour.

We all reach for success. And that imposes an almost pathological faith and belief in the occurrence of the possible. Not one in my group said to me at any time: "I try to do my best." They understand that to succeed, you do everything that is necessary, and you do better than your best. We cannot succeed or master this business without discipline. And that means overcoming obstacles.

Success loves problems. Problems are really opportunities in disguise. Waiting only for a bold, innovative approach. The mind, the will, imagination—all generously combined with discipline—can solve the problems. It becomes a profound and determined contest of the fundraiser with himself. If he persists doggedly, it leads to perfection. And success.

John Davis told me that fundraising takes hard work and plenty of it. "I try to figure out what needs to be done, what the priorities are, and then—I do it. At times, this takes extraordinary discipline. Just keeping at it. Without discipline, we can't succeed."

One wag told me that discipline is having the strength and capacity to break a chocolate bar into four pieces with your bare hands, and eat only one piece! Buck Smith said his life is governed by discipline and that he has the will to do whatever needs to be done. John Miltner told me that, "It's so easy to become diverted, to get involved in a hundred things that really have nothing at all to do with raising funds. In our business, production is the key. We've got to keep our sights on that. Making the call—that's the key question. Self-discipline is critical. We must have it. We live by it. Let's face it—so much of our business really walks in the front door. We don't really have a lot do to with it. I'm constantly setting priorities for myself. I need to know what are the most important things that must be done and then I need to have a plan for getting to them. I'm constantly pushing myself. And that takes discipline. You can spend all of your time and energy going to meetings and not getting something done. As far as I'm concerned, that's not what fundraising is all about. Discipline is the key."

The most effective fundraisers, I find, are motivators— men and women who inspire others to give at the very highest level. These inspired fundraisers are typically people of action and words. Buck Smith says that it may not be a case of persuasiveness. The real job is to help donors see greater and greater opportunities.

Being persuasive is an important factor in our success, but it doesn't necessarily mean being a good salesman. Without question, however, it does involve the ability to transform a vision into a donor's action. According to Statue of Liberty officials, it wasn't salesmanship that rebuilt the statue, and it wasn't money. It was hopes and dreams. It's what Quincy Jones calls taking advantage of other people's goose bumps!

Note this well: People do not give to institutions because the organization needs money. They give because people need help. Institutions don't need help and they don't need money. Institutions have answers, solutions. They need funds to translate these solutions into direct responses for people.

I understand that in a concert, Paderewski hit a lot of wrong notes, yet he somehow managed to move his audience dramatically. Some say that Theodore Dreiser had shabby technique and wrote awkward prose—but was still a distinguished writer despite this. The analogy in the art of fundraising is clear. A lot of great technicians are in fundraising and at times, they even talk the best game. They know all the rules. But there's one rub. Fundraising is persuasion, and persuasion is not a science, but an art. Fundraising is the art of persuasion.

Great fundraisers make great things happen. They incite others to higher aspirations and they motivate larger gifts. The great fundraisers are all visionaries. They see the mountains, not the molehills. To them, the glass is always half-filled, not half-empty. They are visionaries with great capacity for persuasion. They develop effective strategies and imaginative designs. Never ordinary, never mundane.

When Aeschines spoke, they said: "How well he speaks, what glorious words, what magnificent execution." But when Demosthenes spoke, they shouted: "Let us march against Philip." Now, that is true motivation!

Our work follows no immutable laws. It is never predictable. There are machines that can cut a piece of steel to ten-thousandth of an inch and the machine does that every time, consistently right. But fundraising is not like that. It involves people and because of that, it carries with it all of the faults and frailities, and the unpredictability.

Great fundraisers have the glorious capacity to touch the heart and set the stands roaring. They don't do that by salesmanship. It is in having people capture your vision, and make it their own. The great ones pull rather than push people on.

Vartan Gregorian told me a wonderful story. He said: "I sell the institution. I sell the mission. I never ask people for money because we need money. I talk about what a great institution the library is.

"One day I was having dinner with my wife. We were off in a corner in a quiet restaurant. A lady came rushing over to our table and pulled up a chair. I recognized her. She is a woman of immense wealth. And she says to me: 'How come you never ask me for money?' I told her that the library does not need money. But we do need wonderful friends like her who are willing to make it an even greater institution. Before she left our table, she gave me a magnificent check."

John W. Gardner said that fundraisers don't invent motivation or thrive on salesmanship. They unlock what is already there on the part of the donor. Father Hesburgh said: "I think that one of my strengths is my ability to motivate people. I can get them to expand their thinking, to dream bolder dreams." Bruce Heilman said: "You can be a charmer, you can be one of the nicest persons in the world. You can have everything else, but if you can't motivate people, you'll never be a fundraiser. I suppose that is one of the most important ingredients."

Technical skills are primarily concerned with working with "things." Writing copy for a folder, developing a proposal for a grant, understanding direct response mail, purchasing precisely the right software for your computer. These are important, but usually at a lower level in the development office. The ability to motivate is concerned with helping prospective donors jump over fences they never thought possible. That's what motivation is all about.

John Miltner feels that the ability to motivate is a quality that can be learned. "I really think you can work at learning to motivate people. I read about it all the time. I go to sessions about it. I select role models. I look for people who do a good job of motivating others and I try to emulate them. There are born leaders who know how to motivate people. But in my judgment, these skills can be learned and I really work at it."

John D. Rockefeller, Jr., said that the ability to motivate people can be learned and acquired. "And I pay more for that ability than for any other under the sun."

The ability to motivate is our vision and passion, put into action. It is in insisting that at all costs we help our donors avoid "psychosclerosis"—hardening of the attitudes. We understand that we must not let our prospects take a stand or a position against a proposal. They must keep the issues fluid and open. And then, we help them see the great opportunities. Some do this in wondrous ways. The story is told that in a quiet moment, when the two were alone, John D. Rockefeller asked the president of the University of Chicago, William Rainey Harper, if he would like to take a moment to pray. The prayer dealt entirely with the current deficit of the University!

Mel Brooks tells the story of a middle aged man who has been the despair of his family for years because of his compulsive habit of tearing paper into bits, and then scattering the pieces wherever he went. At great expense, and to no avail, the family dragged the man to the world's most highly renowned psychiatrists. Finally they turned to an obscure but innovative new therapist. With the anxious family looking on, this visionary put his arm around the patient's shoulder and said, "Let's take a little walk." The pair walked from one end of the tiny office to the other, the doctor whispering in the patient's ear. At last they stopped, and the doctor said: "You can take him home. He's cured." A year later, when the habit had not returned, the amazed and grateful family asked the doctor, "What did you tell him?" "I told him," shrugged the miracle worker, "don't tear paper." I am convinced that there are countless in this business who would never be that direct with a prospect, who are unwilling to ask for the gift.

Many of the great fundraisers I spoke with mentioned the same concern. Brian Lurie told me: "I think that there are a lot of people in the business who go through all the motions of doing their job, working at their desk, who really don't like asking for money. I can't imagine that sort of person ever being successful in the field. You've got to learn to ask for the order and you've got to learn loving to do it." And the loving part of that equation comes from believing unreservedly and devotedly in the cause and mission of your institution.

It starts with having a belief in yourself. A belief in what you are doing. If you have this, you have sublime confidence to do what is necessary. The big job.

Finally, our success is measured by getting people to respond. There are times you don't even have to ask a direct question. You present the opportunity to them. They see the vision. They are inspired to move. Motivation isn't salesmanship. It is in helping people understand what must be done. And giving them the opportunity to experience the magical joy of doing it. When that happens, it is glorious.

****

9   Soldier of Change

"Blessed is he who has found his work; let him ask no other blessedness."

—Carlyle

"He who does not live in some degree for others, hardly lives for himself."

—Montaigne

A porter carrying a pail and mop watched, then listened to Isaac Stern, who was on a darkened stage, diligently practicing for his concert the next evening. The porter asked: "Do you do this professionally?" A country fiddler brings joy and talent to his instrument, and at times a remarkable level of skill. Isaac Stern, on his Stradivarius, is something else. My hope in this book is not to clone more Isaac Sterns, but to make more and better fiddlers. Fiddlers who bring passion and joy to their work, and a remarkable level of skill. But let me tell you about one of the Isaac Sterns of our business. No mere fiddler, he!

His name is G.T. Smith. I have never heard him called anything but Buck. I'll never forget my first visit, although I witnessed the same scenario many times since. We were crossing the delightful Quadrangle at Chapman College where Buck Smith is president. Without missing a step, he reached down and picked up a candy wrapper from the manicured lawn, rolled it in a ball, and pitched it into a waste bin. He called every student he passed by their first name, stopped here and there for a handshake, a pat on the back, or a word of encouragement. He loves his students, he loves people. And the business about the candy wrapper, he does indeed have a fetish about that. You see virtually no scraps or bits of trash on the campus. It's part of the pride that Buck insists on from his students. I used the term "insists" advisedly. This unmistakable pride starts with Buck, and it's infectious. Everyone on campus has it—the students, the faculty, the maintenance people, everyone.

He has a compulsion for neatness. He's up at 4:15 in the morning and from the moment his feet touch the floor, his workday begins, and it's intensive. He gets along well on four or five hours sleep at night.

Some would say that his professional career took a decided turn for the worse in 1977. That's when he was demoted from being a development director to becoming a college president! Robert L. Gale, president of the Association of Governing Boards of Universities and Colleges, says that Buck Smith can raise money better than any other college president alive. Buck says: "I don't see myself as raising money. I'm making friends for the college."

When he became president of Chapman, it was one payroll away from bankruptcy. The school was hopelessly in debt and had drawers full of unpaid bills the board didn't know about. For Chapman, it was one minute 'till midnight!

Under Smith's leadership, Chapman has reaffirmed its enterprising spirit and is recognized for the quality of its academic programs and for its financial strength. It has just completed an over-goal campaign for $54 million.

One of the nation's leading observers of American higher education recently commented to the press that Buck is "one of the most extraordinary college presidents in America." He personally—although he would claim no credit for himself—has molded and shaped Chapman into being one of the finest small liberal arts colleges in the country.

He is an inspirational leader and speaker. He is equally effective in front of a group or in a one-to-one situation. He is one of the few men I have ever met who can reminisce about the future! He's an exciting person to be around and he somehow manages to transmit this vision and excitement to donors.

He was born in Newton, Mississippi, a town of several thousand people. There were 13 in his graduating class at high school. He did his undergraduate work at the College of Wooster, at the time an institution with 1100 students.

Behind his warm facade is steel of purpose and mission. When he speaks, you have the feeling that he not only wrote the Gospel, he preaches it to the heathen. He understands full well what it means to be on stage at all times. You watch his students, and you know that it is Buck Smith who sets the example, prescribes the pace. He feels that all of us are greatly shaped and fashioned by the things we love. By the people around us. By their inspiration and influence. He considers it one of his prime responsibilities to be a role model.

His achievements at Chapman are monumental, but he is modest to the extreme and doesn't like talking about them. He eschews the limelight and seeks no credit at all. He enjoys his place behind the throne, not on it. The great doyen of fundraising, Harold J. Seymour, said: ". . . to claim credit is to lose it, and to disavow credit often gets you more than you may deserve."

Buck brings an unusual dedication and driving energy to his work. A crusading ardor, a contagious evangelism. That's very likely the term most appropriate to describe Smith—an evangelistic fundraiser.

We were talking one day, and with the conviction that is so typical of him, he said: "I think there's a Biblical reference for development people. God has not given us the spirit of fear— what he has given us is the power of love and sound mind." He said that in fundraising, 95 percent is psychological and spiritual. Only five percent is financial. He doesn't ask people for money, it's almost always the other way around. People come to him and ask what they can do to help. I've seen it happen.

He never lets up. "I have this almost total obsession with quality—with doing things well. If it's worth doing, it's worth doing well. Otherwise, don't spend your energy or resources on it." But he is quick to point out that it is not enough to simply do things well. It is imperative to do the *right* things well.

His ability to involve trustees and donors is legend. "Trustees get those ghastly lectures about their fundraising responsibilities. That is all wrong. The trick is to make involvement so personally rewarding and fulfilling for trustees that they end up asking what they can do to help. It works the same way for donors. And the way to do that is through the use of compelling people and ideas."

Buck Smith is very clear about his role at Chapman: "You don't need a president to run a weekly staff meeting. That's why we have administrators. The role of the president is to raise money." He asserts that we in this business have to bear in mind that people don't give to institutions—they invest in ideas and dreams.

Most of all, one of the strongest impressions you have of Buck Smith is his unfailing love and concern for people. This is what motivates him, keeps him going, from early in the morning until midnight. This love and concern is his fuel. And I find this same attitude in all of the great fundraisers I interviewed. Without this love and concern, this devotion to people, I really don't see how you can be great in this business.

People. The love of people. I listened as my great fundraisers spoke of their concern for people. Genetic or acquired, conscious or not, this concern and love undergirds all they do and is the kindling that fires their success.

Life is a magnificent, rollicking experience. Each of us makes choices, paths that we choose for our life and our work. Living is nothing more than making one conscious decision rather than another. If the choices are right, life should be in the words of Auntie Mame—a smorgasbord. A wonderful and delicious variety.

For most of us, we choose this profession, intentionally or otherwise, because of our love and concern for people. I am certain that the giants in this business receive their inspiration from knowing that they are either saving lives or changing lives. That's what makes all of the frustrations and temporary failures bearable.

Fundraisers were not created to be bystanders. Allowing life to unfold willy-nilly is for us the height of repugnance. We abhor the role of the onlooker. Our dictum is: Life must be lived. We are not spectators in the game. We are the coach, the captain, the players. We thrive on playing each position! When the time has come to play the game, we are ready. Nothing spurs us on to greater peaks of achievement than our concern for people.

"My only motivation in this business is my concern for people," says Father Hesburgh. "There isn't anything that I do outside of this concern. That's what my fundraising is all about. Everything I am and everything I do is because of this concern." Brian Lurie says that you have to touch people. "You have to reach out. There has to be a great love affair with people. I don't think it matters whether you are an extrovert or an introvert— but to be really good in this business, you have to have an enthusiasm about life and a deep concern for people."

They all mentioned it. John Davis told me he was aware of people, no matter where he was or what he was doing. His whole life centers around helping people. "I couldn't be in this business if I didn't have a great concern. I think I know where to push and where to pull. Where and when to provide assistance. If I have any talent at all in fundraising, it is out of this concern." Milton Murray was adamant on the subject. He said that you simply could not succeed if you did not have a concern for people. "There's got to be an element of concern for people. If you don't have it, you can't possibly be successful. It simply can't be done. Those of us in this business have to have a concern for how we affect the lives of people. It's a direct relationship, a direct line. I wouldn't be in this business if I didn't have a real concern for people."

If I had to identify it, I would say it was close to ministerial, this concern and love. My inspired fundraisers all spoke about it. It is hard for me to believe that you can be successful in this field without it. Without this concern, I am certain you will not be an Isaac Stern, and I doubt that you will even be a decent fiddler!

Vartan Gregorian told me that he felt one of his great strengths was his compassion and love for people. "I thrive on people. I really care for people. I care greatly. And I think it shows. I find this work irresistible because of my devotion to people."

Milton Murray is quite clear that it is far more than a case of just liking people. He says that he gets upset if someone tells him that fundraisers are in this business because they "like" people. It's not a back-slapping business we're in, he points out. If you're only in it because you like people, you can work at a department store or be a tour guide at Disneyland. What counts in this business is caring for people. Boone Powell, Sr. says it's imperative that you have a strong humanitarian commitment, possibly a religious motivation.

Buck Smith says that the most important quality he brings to his position is his strong commitment to the college and what it does for people. "I really believe in what I do. Most of the major gifts I've gotten have come because of my strong belief in the college. And this has a direct relationship to my concern and love for people." And Father Hesburgh sent out the strongest signal: "I have never met a successful fundraiser who didn't have a great concern for people. If this doesn't exist, he shouldn't be in the business."

Jim Bowers talked about the passion. "If we lose sight of the person who needs our help, we're useless as a fundraiser. I don't think you can be effective in this business if you don't care a great deal about people. Otherwise, you're just going about your business mechanically and if that's the case, you can't be successful. There has got to be a certain passion."

Theodore Roosevelt said that the most important single ingredient in the formula of success is a concern for people. Whether we realize it or not, this concern for people probably governs everything we do in our work, our attitude, and our results.

I believe that most fundraisers are optimistic by nature. Their attitude is usually upbeat and positive. I have never known a successful fundraiser who spends much time in hand-wringing, complaining about conditions, worrying, or feeling sorry for himself. If you're preoccupied with problems rather than consumed with opportunities, you will never reach the top. And enthusiasm plays an important part. That doesn't mean that you have to be a cheerleader, whipping up enthusiasm at the drop of a siss-boom-bah. It's the genuine enthusiasm for your job and for your life, your concern for others. That's what pays off.

Each chapter of this book deals head-on with the matter of success. It's important because it is everything that we're about. There would be no reason to be in this business, if we didn't strive for success. Someone once said that there are four things that never turn out to be as high as we had hoped—a cathedral, your favorite player's batting average, the crest of a wave, and a dancer's leap. But in our field, we can measure success, and we know how high is high.

George Gallup, Jr. has written a fascinating book on success (*The Great American Success Story*). He says one of the lessons is that anyone can be a success. But note this: Gallup believes that most people write their own script, for some a scenario that automatically assigns them to the status of an also-ran. Yet, most of us in this business have the potential to be high achievers.

Gallup says you can't rationalize the success of others by offering excuses such as: "She always gets all the breaks" or "That organization could raise money no matter who the fundraiser was." Success is within the grasp of each of us. Simply take the steps necessary to achieve it. Some may not wish to make the sacrifice—and in the end, these people may all be happier for it. But if you want to be successful, write your own life's script.

I take strong exception to Santayana who said that one must always be prepared for the worst. There is the theory that if you expect the very worst, you will never be disappointed. Wrong! That attitude will sink you. When you go after the gift, you've got to feel that you will secure it. Conceive it, and you will achieve it. For our work, I say Santayana is wrong. Instead, I believe emphatically that without necessarily being a cock-eyed optimist, be prepared for the very best. And if you are, you will achieve it. Those Santayana pessimists—they are like wingless eagles. Perhaps majestic, but they will not fly.

If you have a difficult undertaking, if you have a really serious problem, if adversity is staring you in the face and the odds are 100 to 1 against you—that's good! Adversity generates inspiration. It gets the juices flowing. You've got a problem—that's good! There is no better environment in which to create a successful, penetrating strategy. Let the juices flow, annihilate those negative thoughts, roll up your sleeves, and get to work. What is required is a firm and steady spirit. The will to succeed. A permanent and self-renewing inner compulsion. Be one with Ben Sweetland who said that success is a journey, not a destination.

The inspired fundraisers love to compete. They thrive on the sense of battle. They love to get into the thick of a confrontation. But mostly, what spurs them on are the plans and actions required to exceed themselves. They don't play against anyone else, they play against par. They know others are going after the same funds and that provides the incentive. But most of all, their great devotion and dedication is to better their own previous best. They understand that they must grow or go. The premiere fundraisers never run out of ideas. They never run out of challenges. They know that they must continue to develop. They can identify with the Nike running shoe poster that says: "There is no finish line."

There are the moments. Those great unexcelled moments. Your spirit soars. You have met your budget. You have captured the gift. You have it all. Lord, right now you could pull the sword out of the stone!

If success isn't important to you, you shouldn't be in this business. The will, the drive, the unrelenting effort to win. And this takes hard work. Without question, Art Linkletter, the great show business personality, is an overachiever in a variety of activities. In his book, *Yes, You Can*, he attests to his inner-drive. He calls it his "Rule of Ten." If anything is worth attempting at all, it is worth trying at least ten times. Then if you're still not succeeding on the eleventh try, reevaluate your technique or drop the project all together. As Schuller said, it may be the wrong dream.

Success means work. Picasso once said that work is the ultimate seduction. Obsessive, brilliant, dedicated—the work-aholic is an extraordinary mixture. I find that in our field, these workaholics don't distinguish work from pleasure. They are men and women, all sizes and shapes, all ages—and they're happiest when they are getting virtually no sleep and working a minimum of a 72-hour week. A relaxing vacation is anathema, impossible to consider. They don't enjoy leisure. Their fund-raising is their leisure. Most haven't taken an extended vacation in years. They are addicts, high on their work. But they are bright, alert, and unbelievably happy. They thrive on their skiddy track, fast-paced work environment. I find that they tend to be terribly demanding, poor delegators of work, and perfectionists to a fault. But there is good news: They are having a wonderful time!

Sean O'Casey said that he found life enjoyable, enchant-ing, active, and sometimes a terrifying experience—and he enjoyed it all immensely. Boone Powell, Sr. says that if you don't love the work, if you don't believe in it, you simply can't be successful. For some, the passion of our profession has changed—from commitment to becoming a duty, the last stage of purgatory. It becomes a burden, a falling away, a gradual surrender of the dream.

These are the unfortunate ones. Uninspired and unexcep-tional, they plod and stumble. They will not know the excite-ment and exhilaration of victory. To them, everything is impos-sible. But we know that whenever something fires the soul, impossibilities vanish. To miss the joy of one's life in fundrais-ing, to miss the exhilaration—is to miss it all.

One of the giants I talked with said that he seldom thought about fundraising—not more than 18 or 19 hours a day! For most of us, getting the gift you are seeking, getting a gift at the right level—it is the consummate joy. Emily Dickinson said: "I know it is poetry if I feel as if the top of my head has taken off." That's about it! That's the sensation I'm talking about.

Nietzsche said that we should make our life and our vocation a matter of play and fun. For some, the great tragedy may be the unused life, the unfulfilled dream. The great danger is that we may finish our life without actually having lived it. That we may come to the end, never having experienced life. Never hearing the call. You can be whatever you want. But only if you choose your life's script and pattern.

For the great fundraisers I interviewed, the joy and exhilaration is in the chase. From the very beginning when the research is developed to, finally, the gift. And then the ultimate—when the gift comes in higher than you thought possible, at an amount which challenged the donor and made him proud. For these great fundraisers, it fills their minds and souls. It is a celebration, a glorious feeling of being one with the universe. And tomorrow, they are thirsting for the challenge of still another contest.

Brian Lurie says that to be an effective fundraiser, you have to be naive. "By that, I mean you have to have pure love, you have to feel it is a wonderful world, you have to be a believer. You have to feel that you can make a difference, a real difference. You have to believe that the world will be a better one and that you can make a contribution to making it so. You have to believe that right will conquer wrong. That man is good. That you can make a difference. That your institution makes a difference."

Being successful—there may not be any secret to it at all. If you believe in the mission of your institution and you love your work, and you do the right things at the right time, and keep persistently at it—there is every possibility you can be successful.

The great fundraisers make their work a journey, and the journey is an ebullient one. Every task is an adventure. Joseph Epstein, in his *Portraits of Great Teachers*, describes how the really great ones love what they do and are passionately involved in their work. They create a sense of drama, excitement, intensity, and exuberance.

Joe Louis once said: "I don't actually like the money, but it sure does ease the nerves." Cosimo de Medici enticed Cellini, the Florentine sculptor, to enter his service by writing him a letter which concluded: "Come, Cellini, I will choke you with gold." But for most of the inspired performers I know, their reward is in their work. They are not in the business because of the money. They are changing and saving lives. That is their reward. This has no direct bearing on the clattering and clang of the coin. The lure of the zeros is simply not great.

Karl Wallenda, the great aerialist, said that being on the tightrope is living—everything else is nonexistence. He died only a few days after making that statement. At age 76, he fell from his high wire. As was his custom, he used no safety net. The world was horrified but it occurred to me that he likely died doing what he loved most, and what he did best. For him, it must have been a glorious end. We in fundraising, we walk this high wire every day, and almost always without a safety net. We are good at our work because we love it.

It is partly a reflection of our positive self-regard. The work propels and compels us on. We love the adventure—yes, even the danger. We are proud of what we do. We have an absolute joy for our work because of our zest for life.

The exhilaration of getting the gift, there is nothing like it. After all of the careful planning, the strategy, the wrenching waiting, the gift finally comes in. And it brings with it an exhilaration unbounded, an elevation of the spirit. The agony has been worth it. We have walked the high wire.

"I love calling on people," says Milton Murray. "I miss it if I'm not doing it. You shouldn't be in this business if you don't love it. For me, it fulfills my sense of service to fellow man. I don't think there is anything else that I could be doing. I thought at one time I would be a doctor, but I realized that was not my calling. I know now that I am doing the Lord's work."

Not all those I interviewed would describe their work in such strongly religious terms, but each spoke about their dedication and almost all felt that they were serving their fellow-man best through their profession. Murray told me the story about the physician who is head of development at Harvard University. He changed his career because he cared so much about raising funds for Harvard and felt that through this channel he could best serve mankind. He got started as a volunteer and realized that what he really loved most in life was raising money. That is how he could make his greatest contribution.

"Let's face it. An awful lot of what we do is detail work and a grind." That's John Miltner talking and he went on to describe many of the details that most of us in this business have to confront. Not many of the great ones really enjoy this aspect of the work. John goes on to say: "But when you actually get into fundraising, that's exciting. I really love what I do. I can't imagine doing anything else."

"It's putting the emphasis in the wrong place," says Boone Powell, Sr. He bemoaned the present emphasis on the bottom line, although as an administrator of one of the largest medical centers in the world, he faced that issue every day. "You hear a lot these days about profit-centers, corporate structures, and strategic planning. That's, of course, an essential part of what all of us are involved in. But I'm afraid that we've lost our mission. What we're really in this business for is caring for people and saving lives. That's what we're really about. And that's the part that keeps me going. I love my work and can't imagine doing anything else."

Those I interviewed did not place much importance or spend much time talking about their own success, their physical appearance, their ability to manage time, or their particular magic. They spoke instead about persistence, commitment, and integrity. They spoke about their profession being their ministry.

Most of all, the inspired fundraisers talked about the love for their work. For the dancer, a particularly high leap must bring a renewal of life, an exhilarating breath of immortality. "When a jump works," says Jacques D'amboise, "It feels like forever. I am riding on top of time." For us, it's the same. The crest of a wave. The top peak of a mountain. It feels like forever.

Many of us think of sin as being an act against God or our fellow man. There can be more to it than that. Sin can also be the failure to reach your full potential. Not attempting the great leap. You must reach beyond your grasp, seek the full limits of the possible, and then go beyond. Sin is not working at your highest potential. The unlived life. Standing by the sidelines, watching. The great fundraisers never stop growing, learning, achieving.

What magnificent fun to be engaged in work which can do so much for so many and where our personal contribution counts for so much. Give your will, mind, and heart to each great cause in which you are involved. Though we in this profession represent a diverse group, we are joined together in a calling of tremendous consequence.

Very few in a lifetime are given the opportunity to make such a substantial difference to society. We are bestowed that role and accept the challenge.

The immense good we do diminishes the agony of the long hours and disappointments. There are peaks and valleys, but we remember most the peaks. We glorify the high leaps. We celebrate the barrier-breaking new horizons we make possible. We love our work, and we are sustained and cheered in knowing how immense our contribution is. We are truly the blessed, fortunate enough to be in this business. We are the veritable soldiers of change.

****

10   The Eureka Factor

"Here is Edward Bear, coming downstairs—bump, bump, bump, on the back of his head, behind Christopher Robin. It is, as far as he knows, the only way of coming downstairs, but sometimes he feels that there really is another way . . . if only he could stop bumping for a moment and think of it!"

—Winnie-The-Pooh

"There is a better way. Find it."

—Thomas A. Edison

John Miltner keeps setting new records. He has had a remarkable career in fundraising, and he is only beginning. For five years, he served as executive director of development for the national office of the Boy Scouts of America. He then joined Memorial Sloan-Kettering Cancer Center in New York City as executive director of development. While there, he set a record for a non-building capital campaign by raising $71.2 million against a goal of $67 million. His budget fundraising endeavors also set a record for an institution of its type—$34 million garnered in a 12-month period.

You might think that anyone could raise money for Sloan-Kettering. Just open the transom over the door of the development office and the money and securities will come tumbling down. Wrong! Before and after John, they didn't raise as much. He went from Sloan-Kettering to California where he is now vice chancellor of advancement for the University of California in Irvine. And he is again setting new records.

He has managed to cross lines and establish new standards in three major disciplines—a youth-serving organization, health care, and now higher education. In 20 years of fundraising, he has raised $490 million.

It raises an interesting question. Some of the giants I interviewed have remained in higher education or in health care their entire career. Mostly, they have done this by choice. But many more, have crossed discipline lines, and with distinction. It proves that "learning the language" of a new organization is not a major problem. What really counts is having that magnificent combination of skills, talent, and physical attributes that go into making an inspired fundraiser.

If this be true—and it is—if a museum, for instance, is looking for a really effective fundraiser, it is almost certain that the least important criterion is to seek a person who has museum experience.

Trust me. I am right on this. Look instead for someone with the right mix of qualities. The language of the institution or the discipline can be learned easily. The magic of fundraising cannot.

Even with his variety of experiences, John Miltner has not jumped from one job to another. He has stayed long enough to understand the organization, properly assess the constituencies, and implement a program that leads to success.

Every one of my great fundraisers had sufficient tenure in his or her position to develop a record and do a good job. The man or woman who moves from one job to another simply doesn't have the time to be effective. I know some of these jumpers. You do, too. They spend the first 18 months writing a new set of procedures, throwing out old systems, and selecting new software for the computer—and then they're on their way to another job. Unfortunate the institution that hires one of these meteors—a fleeting flash that turns to stone, and falls with a thump. The organization gets precisely what it deserves—a fallen flash.

John Dolibois is one of the great mavens of alumni and development work, one of the most highly regarded in the field. He spent a productive lifetime at Miami University in Ohio. He says that too many institutions today are looking for "the instant" fundraiser. They want to organize the campaign today, start the calls tomorrow, and reach goal by next month. But he points out that development people need time to get acquainted with their constituencies. He stresses the need for fundraisers to be working with an institution over an extended period. If the commitment is only to your growth, your own personal needs, your instant success, and your immediate title—you will never be a peak performer. Dolibois would find a way to keep people in their positions longer, "at least long enough to begin to enjoy the great satisfaction, the confidence, and the friendships that are the inevitable by-product of successful tenure."

Tenure counts. Stay long enough to do an effective job. It's really the only way. You owe it to yourself and to the profession. And to your institution.

It is apparent that to become the great fundraiser you might be, to reach your optimum effectiveness—you must go through a long period of introspection and self-discovery. The really great ones in this business go through this assessment their entire career. No matter how long they have been at the business, they understand it is possible to change and improve. It is also necessary to change and improve.

This self-evaluation is essential. All of the giants go through it. They are branded with the characteristic of healthy dissatisfaction. They go through life feeling they could do better, should do better. For most, there is isolation and introspection, search and study, churning and challenging. No matter how effective they are, no matter how good a year they've had, they continue to strive—they never cease strengthening and polishing their skills.

The great ones are result-oriented. They invented the term: Bottom line. Every day, they accept this accountability. We all have days of failure. But if we are diligent in our efforts, we know there'll be a new day.

It doesn't just happen. The great fundraisers, they make it happen. The strong ones, there is this awesome commitment to their work. A love affair. Let's face it, at times the dedication is challenged: a new opportunity opens outside fundraising, frustrations occur with a board member, the long hours begin to wear on you. But no matter what seems to happen, the commitment continues and with it, fulfillment and rewards.

Discipline. Hard work. Pleasure postponed. Responsibility completed. These virtues lead to success. Living on the edge. Pressing to the horizon's very rim. Mind and soul merge. This is the exciting life.

Coping, striving, fighting to become the person you are. The final product of a lifetime of dedication, knowing that you are really good at your profession, that you are creating the future. You become lost in the present. In your drive for self-reflection, you discover all.

And you discover, also, that happiness is found not in the pursuit of happiness, but in the achievement of the highest objectives.

Believe in the "Eureka Factor." New ideas are born and thrive in an environment of deliberate receptivity and wild abandonment. Eureka! I've found it. Amid the clinking clutter of dead customs and traditions, obsolete service, outmoded programs—you find it. Eureka! It is a strike of lightning.

Objective logic, blinding data, and thorough analysis will take you only part way down the path to making a decision regarding a prospect. Finally, you have to make an outrageous, perceptive leap. You call on that huge reservoir submerged in the depth of your subconscious. There it is, all ready and waiting for your call—your cumulative knowledge, your experience, and your educated intuition.

Count on it. Rely on it. If you have a very strong feeling that you should do something, have faith in that insightful feeling. Often, you may not be able to come up with a logical and valid argument why it's there waiting for you. Don't worry—just fall back on the "Eureka Factor." Count on it.

Something way down there is telling you what to do, and it's almost always the right choice.

Resolute and purposeful action is required. At some point, you must make a decision. The timing may not be precisely right. It almost never is.

If you wait for perfect timing, you will likely never make the call. If all possible objections must first be overcome, nothing will be attempted. That doesn't mean that you shoot from the hip. But at some point, you must shoot! That's far better than the person who is always aiming, but never willing to pull the trigger. It means taking the risk, departing from old and worn paths, pursuing fresh ideas and innovative activities. Boldness counts. Those of you inclined to fear or failure will find the path in this business filled with anguish and agony.

Expect the unexpected. Indeed, you must probe and pursue the unexpected. You must let yourself be led astray. A new path, a new adventure. You must be totally open and encouraging to the risk of the unforseen. It is only in this way that you will find the great answers. Alexander Graham Bell was trying to invent a hearing aid. Columbus was looking for India. Louis Pasteur, a cure for a disease of the silk worm.

The unimaginative fundraiser is all too common. His work is pedestrian and ho-hum. Creativity requires grit and determination—and an uncommon act of will. It doesn't just happen. It needs to be pursued with relish, and resolve. Fundraising is most often the art of imaginative assuming, the art of intensive conceiving.

Each of my inspired fundraisers placed great importance on innovation. They used the "why not" approach. Why can't it be done? Why not try it this way? Why not try for a larger gift? They practice the credo of "Not If . . . but Why Not?" They understand that fundraising demands innovation and imagination. They talk about the crucial need to work around the edges, test the fringes. Their life is ruled by creative chaos and nurtured by unlimited opportunities.

When you are in fundraising, you are in the idea business.

Brian Lurie says: "One of my great strengths is in creating an idea, providing the vision, and then making it happen."

The great ones abhor uniformity-conformity. Vartan Gregorian says: "I am different. I recognize that. In many ways, this is one of my great strengths. I try to keep a delicate balance between my own individualism and still work within the proper framework of social acceptance. Most important, I look for a different approach to everything. A better way. I free my mind. I am a creative person."

You can't do things differently until you see them differently. Discovery is the act of looking at the same factors, the same research, the same prospect—and then thinking something different.

"Why didn't I think of that?" The best litmus test of a great idea, a new approach, is its simplicity. "Oh, anyone could have gotten that gift if they had gone after it that way." That's the tip-off. Then you know for certain that it's a great idea.

Alfred North Whitehead said that the analysis of the ordinary requires an extraordinary mind. Our job is to dig in our heels and resist the usual. John D. Rockefeller, Jr. spoke to all fundraisers when he said: "If you want to succeed, you should strike out on a new path rather than travel the worn paths of accepted success."

"It's my idea, I stole it first!" Ah, don't fret! That's overstated for effect, but close to the truth. The mediocre borrow, the brilliant steal. Creativity does not mean originality. It means looking at things differently, from a different perspective. A different twist, a new turn. Stretching, reducing.

It is an internal revolution which engenders ferment. It is our unencumbered and unrelenting enthusiasm for the unexplored. Thomas Edison said that he was a good sponge. "I absorb ideas and put them to use. Most of my ideas first belong to people who didn't bother to develop them." Edison did not invent the light bulb. He took someone else's idea and improved it. Over the years, he tried hundreds of filaments before he found one just right for incandescence. He took someone else's idea and improved it. Imagination and innovation rule the world. And blinding persistence.

Peter Drucker compares fundraising to the corporate world and says that only two basic factors lead to success—marketing and innovation. But be ready to face the indifference and resistance that any change provokes. You will be a lonely person! A really new idea at first has only one believer—you. Fanaticism is crucial. Peter Drucker says: "Whenever anything is being accomplished, it is being done by a maniac with a mission."

It is said that what set Thomas Edison apart was that he conveyed the feeling that he would succeed. No matter what obstacles he might face, he would pound away until he had demolished them. Creativity requires untiring inspiration and unflagging fortitude—a maniac with a mission.

If the only tool you have is a hammer, you tend to see every problem as a nail. The great ones have many implements and devices in their tool box, and imagination is one of the most often used. Jim Bowers says: "I work very hard at being creative. I work at it all the time. I think it's one of my strongest attributes. I always have been curious and imaginative. I never seek a single solution to any problem. I try to think of all of the different answers and solutions that may exist."

Edison said that genius is one percent inspiration and 99 percent perspiration. The evidence is that the elements for creativity are a mixture of curiosity, intuitiveness, enthusiasm, and flashing streaks of independence.

A friend of mine at General Electric said to me: "At GE, we never talk about problems, we speak only of opportunities. But there are times that we have a helluva lot of opportunities!" How lucky we are, we fundraisers. We are surrounded by opportunities. At times, we feel we are drowning in them. But how exciting to be able to get up in the morning and attempt to do something about it. That's the exhilaration of our work. Alfred P. Sloan said that when you're through changing, you're through.

When Andrew Carnegie was at the height of his business career, he was interviewed by Napoleon Hill. Carnegie told Hill about a mysterious master power he used in all of his corporate dealings. He called it a magic law of the mind.

There are five steps to Carnegie's Law, each of which can be translated into a development director's focus for success:

1) Fix firmly in your mind the precise amount of money you wish to raise. It is not good enough to merely say "I want to raise a lot of money." Be precise about the amount.

2) Determine what you intend to give in return for reaching your objective. What compromises are you willing to make in your life—working more hours, seeing your family a little less, working in a more organized way, attending fewer meetings, getting to the office earlier and working later, or whatever? There is no such thing as "something for nothing."

3) Establish a specific date when you intend to secure the gifts you desire.

4) Create a definite plan for carrying out your desire. Put it in writing. Then, begin at once, whether you are ready or not, to put the plan in action. This clear, concise statement should include the amount of money you wish to raise, the time limit for its acquisition, and what you intend to give in return for the money. Describe clearly the plan through which you intend to raise it.

5) Finally read your statement aloud twice a day. Read it once just before retiring at night and once again when you get up in the morning. Visualize it, feel it, believe it. Believe that you have already raised the money. Think about it.

Before you dismiss this concept out of hand, try it. I promise you, it works. It worked for Carnegie. It worked for Napoleon Hill. It has worked for hundreds. And it will work for you.

In a recent study George Gallup, Jr., conducted among 1,000 men and women he considered "the most successful in their field," he identified what he considered to be the 12 most important characteristics for success.

Leading the list and considered to be the most important of all characteristics is common sense. An important distinction needs to be made between intelligence and common sense. All of the giants I interviewed are above average in intelligence. I am certain that several are at genius level. Yet not one rated intelligence as being a significant factor in being a great fundraiser.

The great ones in this field have insatiable inner drive and self-confidence. As they say, "The supreme confidence of a Methodist with a Royal Flush!"

The other factors which stand out in an obvious manner are "the strong ability to communicate, the tenacity and organization to get things done, and a dynamic quality of leadership."

With a few exceptions, none I interviewed could truly be called an intellectual. But they were all endowed with immense common sense. All had what I call "copability." No matter what the situation, even if it is the very first time they have encountered a complex dilemma, they are able to cope with it. Nothing throws them. It is what some call "street smart," and all of my people have it. Nothing throws them, nothing is too difficult, every problem is an opportunity. In today's world, common sense is not common at all. Give 50 extra I.Q. points for good common sense!

Good judgement comes from hard fought tough wrought experience. And as they say, experience comes from—bad judgement!

Bruce Heilman said that he felt being intelligent was the least important quality of all. "That doesn't mean that you can be dull—but I know an awful lot of highly intelligent fundraisers who are not good at their job at all." Charles Beacham, the former president of Ford Motors, spoke often about what he called street smarts—the things you just know, the basic lessons that can't really be taught. "The only thing you've got going for you in whatever field you're in, is your ability to reason and your good common sense."

Vartan Gregorian, who almost certainly is at genius level, told me that he felt intelligence was not significant at all. "A

fundraiser must have common sense, an ability to cope immediately with any situation. I don't understand why common
sense is sometimes hailed as revolutionary. I suppose that's
because so few have it."

You and I know some in this field who are like the Platte
River—one mile wide and six inches deep! They rarely say a
foolish thing, nor ever a wise one either. It has nothing to do
with education. Honda boasts only eight years of school. Henry
Ford had even less. Thomas Edison did not complete high
school. A legion of successful men and women never made it
through school. Academic credentials are certainly not the
greatest factor in producing an effective fundraiser. The notion
has occurred to many that the reason the Japanese are so successful is that they don't have any graduate schools of business administration!

Henry Kissinger is reported to have said that he wasn't as
smart as God—"but I'm as smart as He was at my age!" The
story has got to be apocryphal—originated by a Democrat, no
doubt—but it is well documented that Kissinger regularly
recommended "a Secretary for Common Sense" for Nixon's
Cabinet.

Joel P. Smith, formerly head of fundraising at Stanford
University, says that he places high priority on resourcefulness,
not intelligence. He points out that the activities that fundraisers are involved in are so variable, so unpredictable, so basically
impossible to accomplish by formula, that to handle appro-
priately and effectively the array of things that happen, they
must be resourceful. Street-savvy. Bright. Not necessarily intelligent, but endowed with an abundance of common sense.
Intelligence is a part of that, but Smith gives much greater
weight to resourcefulness and common sense. And the ability to
distinguish the urgent from the trivial. The capacity to index
and solve problems are major components of our business, and
this is most effectively done through common sense.

James Hodges Webb was Secretary of the Navy. He is
driven, uncompromising, professional. He graduated first in
his class at Annapolis and commanded a marine company in

Viet Nam. He has more decorations than a wedding cake. He claims that the mark of a true leader in any field is the ability to handle stress and the display of good common sense. Every difficult job possesses physical and psychological problems. A great leader places his experience and common sense against the complexity of the problem.

Father Hesburgh told me: "I don't feel I'm brilliant. Not by any means. I have discovered that you've got to keep learning, learning, learning. You're at it forever. I'm smart enough to know that. I don't think you're going to make it if you're not willing to keep on learning. That, and having a great deal of common sense."

Yeats wrote that poetry was blood, imagination, and intellect brought together. Fundraising is—blood, imagination, and common sense brought together.

Lee Iacocca says that "whenever I've taken risks, it's been after satisfying myself that the research and market studies supported my instincts. But inevitably, I act on my own intuition and common sense."

The ability to conceptualize and see the big picture was considered by all to be of importance, but not necessarily one of the most consequential factors.

Perhaps this is assumed to be a given characteristic, common for all who are successful in the business. It is simply something we should all have, the ability to see the big picture. Looking forward, looking ahead—feeling deep down that you haven't reached your greatest heights. Haven't gone as far as you should. So much more is always to be done. You know you can do better.

Every organization and institution has a variety of problems, quite often in monumental proportions. The successful fundraiser is able to understand the big picture, but is also able to analyze, separate, and untangle the dilemma, and break it into smaller, digestible pieces. For you, you must not see difficulties or problems—only opportunities.

You must maintain rigidity in your schedule so that you're not swallowed by someone's desire for your attention. Not unless that person rates very high in the achieving of your objective. Just make certain you distinguish between an objective and an obstruction. It's fun to chat with an associate over coffee, to be on the phone with a friend, to spend time planning next month's NSFRE meeting. That may be important, but it's not really the payoff.

Some don't really understand the true target. Or they understand it and are unwilling to go after it.

The successful people in this business do not confuse a flurry of activity with effectiveness. They do not allow paperwork to substitute for personal contacts. And they do not permit small problems and details to take the time which should be spent on developing bold long-term plans. Often, sheer activity and busyness are the resting place and refuge of the mediocre.

The ability for focused, uninterruptable concentration is essential if you are to succeed. Add to that the effective and organized use of your time. To know where you are going, to seize the action, and then to put all of your power and might into the plan. That's what assures success. The non-doers, the theorists—they continue to lecture on navigation while the ship is going down.

It takes rigid organization of one's time, and then finally the ability to move, to take action. Ross Perot, the extraordinary entrepreneur, has a special disdain for the non-doer, the man who sits on his . . . well, sits on his hands. Perot points out, also, that this type of person usually won't act on his own, but insists on a decision-by-committee. Perot feels that this strangles an enterprise. He says that for many, their work follows the pattern of "Ready, Aim, Aim, Aim, Aim."

I asked the very efficient secretary to Jim Bowers, Deanna Gibson, to tell me how Jim spends his time. "Give me a typical day, Deanna. I know there's probably none that is typical, but give me an idea of the type of pattern he follows."

She started thumbing through his daily calendar. "They're all frantic. I don't know why the poor man doesn't run away from home!"

We finally found a day that I'll describe. It may be busier than most, but I really can't say for certain. His calendar looked jammed with activity. Understand, also, there are at least 20 to 30 telephone calls a day, endless meetings, staff popping in, and donors and prospects who simply want to come by to say hello and chat.

On the one day we looked at, he had two breakfasts. Two! The first started at seven o'clock, the second at eight-fifteen. Both were meetings with hospital staff.

In the morning, he had a session to plan for the meeting of the board of directors coming up the following week. There followed a meeting with the officers of the auxiliary—"we'd like you to consider a really major project for the coming year. The hospital needs some special equipment . . ." Then he was scheduled to meet with the entire staff to plan for the announcement of a new building to be housed on the hospital campus.

Then, a wild dash to his car and a race to a luncheon meeting where one of his prime donors was being honored by the San Diego Press Club. Strictly speaking, this is not a hospital function, but when a donor gives you $5 million, everything that revolves around him becomes "a hospital function."

Back to the office. Deanna says that in the early afternoon, he usually tries to return half a dozen calls or so. At times like these, you are almost pleased if the other party isn't in. At least you get points for trying. Come on now, you know the feeling.

There are letters to sign, dictated late the evening before. Then off to a meeting of the Candlelight Ball Committee in the conference room of the hospital. That's really been delegated to another member of the staff, but it's important that Jim makes a cameo appearance. It's expected. He greets everyone, asks how Louise's kids are doing, makes an important suggestion—and is off and running, back to his office. A few more phone calls, a couple he initiates and a couple he has to return, and then 30 minutes with Ames Early, the chief executive officer of the hospitals. Jim carries the portfolio for fund-raising and public relations at Scripps, but because of his unusual sensitivity to marketing concerns, he and Ames confer often on myriad topics.

He has time for a quick touch-up with the electric razor before he has cocktails with Edwina and Bob Marvin. The Marvins are great friends of the hospital, strong boosters, and have the potential for a major gift. They live in the Fairbanks Ranch area, just outside of Rancho Santa Fe. Cocktails and a brief visit are just right—Jim has a board meeting at 7:30 at the Fairbanks Ranch Country Club, where he's on the house com-mittee. At last, something strictly personal and social in a hectic day shoe-horned in with hospital activities. Wrong! The coun-try club board involves some of the most influential and afflu-ent men and women in the country. Jim manages to make subtle and skillful points for the hospital.

He is home a little before eleven o'clock, physically drained, and a little overfed. At last, time to relax and prepare for bed. Wrong! There's the day's mail to go through—Deanna had tucked it in his briefcase. And there are a few letters to dictate. And yes, the list of things that he must tackle first thing in the morning.

This really is not an unusual day. And Jim is on the board of the Civic Light Opera and the ballet, an animal shelter, the American Institute of Wine and Food, and a half dozen other agencies. And he's heavily involved in NSFRE, NAHD, and the Public Relations Society. He takes his professional life seriously.

It doesn't leave a lot of time to raise money!

Let Father Hesburgh, in his own words, tell you what one of his days is like. He did not choose an unusual day—they're all like this. He says that: "The only way you can accomplish a lot is to concentrate on the task you have at hand at the moment. Otherwise, you go nutty.

"Yesterday, I was down in New Orleans. I had everything cleaned up before I left on Sunday, except the unfinished reading on the window sill." You can always tell the extent of Father's work schedule and his travel by the depth of the reading material on his window sill! A few inches and you know he's pretty much caught-up and has been on campus. It has been known, however, to grow beyond several feet and two piles deep. You know Father is in trouble!

"I took everything I could pack in my bags, and read an awful lot of stuff along the way. Then I came back and the stack was two feet high. And lots of phone calls to return. But eventually you catch up. You just have to remember that.

"I was reading the Bishop's statement on the airplane, pretty significant stuff. Then coming home, I had people coming in who I just had to see—the head of the alumni board on a problem with black alumni and how to get more black kids into school, a couple of company officials coming in to give us a check; you've got to spend a little time with them and talk about their project and how it is going.

"In the midst of all this, I was absolutely shaggy, so I said 'Whatever happens, get me a barber!' At five o'clock I ran to the barber and must have gotten stopped four or five times enroute by kids, but that's just fun. They wanted to ask me something nutty, so I gave them some nutty answers, and we laughed about it.

"I got the haircut, ran back—I'd been gone for three days—was up at six o'clock yesterday in New Orleans to catch the plane back here in time to say mass at 11:30, which I did." Father Hesburgh says mass everyday, wherever he is, on campus or in some remote part of the world.

The rest of the afternoon was spent in one activity after another—faculty, the financial officer, a parent, one meeting followed another until dinner time.

"I had to break a long standing appointment in order to have dinner with some top Chinese students I had first met in China. I had promised we'd get together, but I was still mindful of that two-foot stack of mail on my desk. I had to find out what was in it and after glancing at it, I had to consult with some people, and I remembered that I had a bad week coming up as

I've got to go again to New York to help select a new president of the Council on Foreign Relations and I knew I had to go through that stack of candidates, every sheet.

"But instead of doing anything else, I went out and had a four hour Chinese dinner with these guys, because you can't do a Chinese dinner right in less time than that . . . four hours later, I came back here, finished reading the stack of resumes and got to the bottom of that mail pile, and those letters that had to get out right away—and they were here to sign when I returned this morning. When I quit at 2:30 in the morning, the out-box was piled pretty high."

Father Hesburgh has maintained that sort of a schedule every day, year in and year out, since he was named president of the university in 1952. If he feels any stress, he doesn't show it. He appears totally in control. It's obvious, he loves what he's doing. He loves every moment and, of course, it is his ministry. But for all of us in this profession, helping to change lives and save lives, it is our ministry.

In talking about his schedule, Father Hesburgh says: "But the whole point is that the world doesn't stop, you have to roll with it and not get excited about it." A thoughtful pause, and then: "Let me correct that, the world doesn't stop, and you should get excited about that."

All of the successful fundraisers I know maintain a similar schedule—frantic, frazzled, and frenzied. And they thrive on it! I'm not saying that's right for everyone. It's not. But success means hard work, long hours, and uncompromising endurance.

Take John Miltner as another example. Almost all I interviewed have pretty much the same sort of schedule, but look at what John considers a typical day. He starts his work day at the office at seven o'clock, unless he has a breakfast meeting. He leaves the office at 6:30 p.m. Most evenings he has commitments—social and professional which involve the university.

He tries not to take work home, but he does! Most evenings, however, he does his reading. And its prodigious. Three newspapers everyday, from beginning to end. Every day! Fifteen to 20 magazines every month—not necessarily cover-to-cover. But he's a compulsive reader—everything that comes his way professionally, and then some personal reading.

How exciting. How wonderful to be head over heels involved in work that is driving and demanding. If there weren't the problems and the stress, if there wasn't the daily race, life would be a bowl of pabulum.

It takes organization. Organization and action. A good plan executed with gusto, consummated on the spot, is far better than a perfect plan executed sometime "in the near future." Procrastination is the art of keeping up with yesterday. To be successful in this field, everything depends on action—and that means the meticulous planning and organization of your time.

In Alec Mackenzie's *The Time Trap*, he says that time is irreplaceable. "It cannot be accumulated like money or stock, piled like raw materials. We are forced to spend it whether we choose to or not, and at a fixed rate of 60 seconds every minute. It cannot be turned on and off like a machine or replaced like a man. It is irretrievable."

Time. To those of us in this business, there is no single commodity more precious. It is the raw material of everything. It governs everything we do. Our success. Our life.

If we organize properly, all things are possible. Without effective structure, nothing. It is the miracle of each day, the inexplicable prize we each have. We wake up in the morning, and our treasure chest is magically filled with 24 hours. For the proper use. There are interruptions, the unexpected moments, the bothersome phone call, the letters to be signed, the staff person who needs just a moment of your time. For those who are among the most effective, every moment is a glorious jewel, to be savored, polished, and carefully stored. Pity the fundraiser who throws away any portion of his allotted 24 hours.

The seconds pass, the clock ticks, the race goes on. Even the turning of the calendar page causes a sense of anxiety and urgency.

The great fundraisers are time-compelled. Articles need to be written, meetings attended, calls made. Income budgets must be met and capital campaigns must be won.

Meet. Run. Leap. Win. The race goes on each day. For those who organize properly their allotted 24 hours, the world is theirs.

Some days it just doesn't seem worth it: Press on. You're not feeling at top form: Keep going. It's four o'clock, easy to slip out: Keep working. The world is won by those who are willing to make one more call.

The typical fundraiser is not unlike most business and corporate executives—harried and hurried. We face the minutia-drenching bits and pieces of routine—and have no one to turn to. We come to the end of a day weary, worried, and worn. We haven't done everything we hoped. We ran short of time. Our day was filled with staff, stupidity, and stuff. Good grief, where did the day go? We drown in details. We fail to take time to organize, to coordinate, and to carry forward. Our institution treads water, waiting for us to achieve high levels of success. But we face day after day a stack-filled desk top of work. Taking care of all of this detail and work is a horrendous burden. We simply don't have time to call on anyone for a gift!

To get it done requires organization and action. The "wait-till-tomorrow" syndrome simply is not good enough. It's no more successful than trying to leap a deep chasm in two bounds. This all may seem obvious, but it isn't always practiced.

Discipline, that is important. In the case of some fundraisers, ambitions and egos are so immensely enormous that they endanger the results. With this kind of a personal sense of urgency, there is the tendency to burst to conclusions at merely the slightest spark of evidence. They move too quickly before the prospect is truly in sight. They aren't on target. They don't reach the right conclusions—much like the determination that if mice are experimented on regularly, they will develop cancer!

John Masters is head of one of the world's most successful oil and gas wildcatter firms. He says: "This is so simple it sounds stupid, but it is amazing to me how few oil people understand that you only find oil and gas when you drill wells. You may think you're finding it when you're drawing maps and studying logs, but you have to drill. That takes action, and that takes proper organization of your time. If you have both of those, you'll find oil."

You've seen them and so have I. Some in our business start slowly and then sort of taper off. They have no enchantment or enthusiasm for their work. They stumble and fall. The chief objective of a fundraiser is to see how it can be done rather than why it cannot be done. That is the mission.

Much of this business is routine, dull, and grubby. But routine and the organization of one's time is the momentum that fuels our days.

Finding the inspiration is not a strike of lightning. You have to work for it. If you wait to be inspired, you'll be standing on the sidewalk, and the parade will pass you by.

The mediocre fundraiser somehow manages to get by. In 18 months, he may even get a new job offer. I've seen these folks move from spot to spot, and usually with an increase in pay. Blessed are the executive search firms! But these 18-month wonders are not an asset to either themselves or the institution. The good fundraiser does well and is a credit to the institution. The superior fundraiser is filled with the excitement and exhilaration of his work. Each day is an adventure. But the really great fundraiser, he is an inspiration.

This business has it all. It is everything. An ever changing, wild and wonderful, living thing. Building to glorious peaks—somehow diminishing the memory of the low valleys and disappointments. Just like in golf, you tend to remember only your good shots!

The soul and spirit of fundraising is a beguiling blend of needs and desires, grind and gratifications. The alchemy of sacrifice and personal contribution goes far beyond any material reward we could hope for. This business, it is the ultimate venture. Those who are inspired and successful in the field live each day as the wildest of all explorations. The chance to catch a close view of things seen never before.

****

11   You Start with Integrity

"To overcome difficulties is to experience the full delight of existence."

—Schopenhauer

"If you have something difficult to do, don't expect people to roll stones out of your way."

—Dr. Albert Schweitzer

One of my lasting memories of Milton Murray is of a late evening flight I took on a blustery February day. I arrived at Chicago's O'Hare Airport past midnight. I was the picture of the worn and weary traveler. Unkempt, rumpled suit, and beaten to the bone.

Coming off the plane, I spotted Milton in the waiting room, surrounded by papers. A worn, bulging leather briefcase by his side, overflowing. He had one of those long yellow tablets he was writing on, whistling and working. He was obviously having a magnificent time, doing what he enjoyed most—working. Oblivious to everyone, he was up to his elbows in paper and work. No lost time, no lost motion. I touched his shoulder and broke the concentration. Ten minutes of uninterrupted discourse followed on his latest pet-project. There's always a pet-project. He makes even a workaholic like me feel lazy. He's an inspiration. I left, feeling ten feet tall.

Dr. Milton Murray is the coordinator and director of all philanthropic endeavors for the Seventh-day Adventist Church. With the force of a speeding train, he directs, coordinates, cajoles, and provides a great deal of love to several hundred Adventist universities and schools, hospitals, and medical centers. He has the magnificent countenance of a swan—to the view of all, majestic and calm. But below the surface, paddling like crazy!

The other night I was on the West Coast, and received a telephone call around eleven o'clock. It was Milton.

"Milton, it's wonderful to hear from you. I'm going to be around here for a couple days, are you on the Coast?"

"No, I'm calling from home, in Washington,"

"Good grief, Milton. It must be two in the morning. What the devil are you doing up?"

"I had ten minutes to myself and I just thought I'd say hello." And then followed a long conversation about two things that he cares dearly about these days—his magnificent calendars and his untiring effort to get the post office to issue a commemorative stamp for philanthropy. He figures that he is going to get the stamp issued and "it will only take another three years or so." Three years! Most of us don't plan beyond next week.

He speaks with great pride and affection about his father: "A tough administrator but a warm and open-hearted man and minister. He was a great influence on my life." Virtually all of the great fundraisers I spoke with talked to me about someone in their life who was a great influence, who managed to get deep underneath their skin, who changed their life forever. Most of these models and childhood influences helped form the framework of integrity, which is characteristic of those I talked with.

Take Anita Rook as another example. She is leading a $50 million campaign for the National 4H Clubs. She's as savvy and effective as any in the business. Her father was a minister in the Church of God and held a variety of posts, all in small cities. Anita grew up in a village in Indiana. One hundred graduated in her class from Oglethrope College. "I owe my whole value system to my father. He was a great influence on me. He really made me think, think and act about those things which are important to me."

I asked Milton once if he thought he was a workaholic. He said he probably is. "The truth of the matter is, my wife gets a little disturbed with me at times. I might be away for a very busy and hectic week, come in the door, and then head right for the telephone and start making calls. She's been wonderful through all the years, and extremely understanding." It does, indeed, require an understanding spouse.

Most of those I interviewed have been happily married for years. Several were divorced and remarried, and a few remained single but married to their job.

I have known Milton Murray for more than 20 years, and I consider him one of the great spirits in this business. The contribution he has made, his influence on thousands, his extraordinary sense of integrity—all of this is of incalculable value. May his tribe increase.

It would be difficult to identify what stands out most about the man but I think those who know Milton would agree it's his integrity. It glows—as a beacon. The same characteristic is common in high proportions with all the great ones with whom I spoke.

Integrity forms the foundation for everything we do and all that we are. Peter F. Drucker is America's recognized guru of management. He says that the ultimate requirement of effective leadership is to earn trust—otherwise, there won't be any followers. "Trust is the conviction that the leader means what he says. It is a belief in something very old-fashioned called integrity." He coud have been speaking to fundraisers.

Integrity is not negotiable. Integrity isn't the most important thing—it is everything.

I have referred throughout this book to Vartan Gregorian. He was born in the Armenian quarter of the northern Iranian city of Tabritz. His mother died when he was six and he was raised by his grandmother. She had a profound influence on his life. "She taught me that the only things in life that are really important are your dignity and your integrity." He spoke with great feeling about his grandmother and reminisced about those early days.

Then he got back to the subject of integrity: "For a fund-raiser, nothing is more important than integrity and dignity. This must be at the top of the list. People know that when I speak, what I say is straight. Always direct and the truth. It is because of my great respect for individuals. I would never, for instance, think of urging people to make a gift if it was against their will. My job is to make the gift something that will be of inspiration and need to them. Self respect means respect for others. It all revolves around integrity."

Father Walsh is the former president of Boston College. He later became president of Fordham University. We were in his car, driving to his club for dinner. He said something to me that made such an extraordinary impact that I pulled out my pen and a card and wrote it down. "Integrity is what you have left when everything else you have ever been taught is forgotten."

All of the qualities, skills, and characteristics I have written about are essential to have in the fundraiser's basket. But if you had to put all your eggs in one, it would be the "integrity basket." Integrity is quintessential. It is the soul and marrow of the fundraiser.

It wasn't always this way. The early fundraisers, according to one admittedly exaggerated recollection, owe their lives "to the fact that there was a law against killing them!" Some who don't really know us say that fundraisers have always been given to the improvising of life-long convictions. A person who bamboozles one party and plunders the other. Robert Benchley said that it took him a long time to discover that the key to good fundraising is honesty and integrity. Once you know how to fake that, you've got it made!

Thankfully, we in this business typically have a healthy sense of humor. We can handle these gibes and jests in the same way we throw off golf stories. I suspect that there was a time, years ago, when a few in the business operated in an Alice in Wonderland of unfounded claims, impossible promises, fancy packages, soaring words, and sheer puffery. That would not only be unacceptable in today's world, it simply wouldn't work.

Among the effective fundraisers, there is a blazing streak of Presbyterian moralism. I told Bruce Heilman that what impressed me most when I heard him speak to donors of the university was the deep conviction and straightforward approach he took. The presentation wasn't fiery. That wouldn't be Bruce's style. But it was eloquent and inspirational. Most of all the integrity of the man shone with brilliance. He said: "I think the people I call on trust me, they believe what I tell them. This kind of relationship takes time and it takes integrity. I can't imagine a really great fundraiser without integrity. If you don't have it, people will find you out." George Engdahl told me that a myriad of characteristics and skills are important but that the greatest of these is integrity. It is basic, a starting point.

For most, it isn't something you talk a great deal about. Buck Smith says that integrity is a given. It is in a class by itself. "It's the number one thing I look for in someone. The great ones in fundraising I have known are never willing to compromise principle for result. It is easy to take advantage of someone and I can't tolerate that."

Robert Schuller said that at the top of his list—he puts integrity. "Integrity of the person, integrity of the idea, and integrity of the program. Money is attracted to ideas that have urgency and integrity."

You cannot separate good fundraising from integrity. It is not as easy when Fitzgerald said to Ernest Hemingway: "You're a great writer, Hem, but you're a very bad person." No one would accept the premise that you can be a really great fundraiser and be lacking in integrity. W.A. Criswell says: "You start with integrity. That's the beginning. Every great fundraiser must have it."

Almost certainly, this is the single most important quality in any field of human endeavor. Integrity does mean different things to different people. There's the story of a lady who goes into a store and makes a purchase and doesn't realize that she has given the owner two $20 bills stuck together. To him, integrity isn't whether he gives one of the $20 bills back to the lady—the question is whether he should split it with his partner! We may understand the humor in that story, but not the message. Integrity is the characteristic which glues the fundraiser to his organization and the prospect. It is a quality that cannot be forced or bought.

In every field that has meaning and interaction, integrity is essential. Peter Drucker says it is the most important quality of leadership. Frank Lloyd Wright said: "What is needed most in architecture is the very thing that is most needed in life—integrity." The same can be said of fundraising. The former magician of marketing for IBM, Buck Rogers, said that those who hope to be successful over the long term in any field need the cooperation, loyalty, and respect of others. "The people of integrity don't compromise, they keep their promises, meet their commitments, live their values, and strive their utmost. But most of all, it's integrity."

Father Hesburgh says: "There's absolutely no substitute for integrity. Nothing can take its place. You can't be a fundraiser without it." And W.A. Criswell told me that the bedrock of our work must be integrity. That is the foundation. When I showed him a list and asked him to rate the ten most important qualities of a fundraiser, he said—integrity is numbers one through ten!

Joel P. Smith says that effective fundraisers, to be truly successful, must have personal integrity. No short cuts, no end-runs. "My own feeling about personal integrity is that it is far, far more impressive when it is demonstrated by behavior. I am unimpressed by people who talk continually about their own integrity." He says that integrity ought to be implicit rather than explicit. He suggests that our clients and prospects read us. Read us extremely well. Let the fundamental commitment to integrity be implicit. "But let us make sure the commitment is there, because there isn't any way to succeed, or to be highly regarded, or to deserve self-respect unless we subscribe to the highest standards of personal integrity."

Integrity was not on my original list. When I made up my initial group of skills, talents, and characteristics, there were 96 items. I wanted to narrow it to a third the number. I did that by talking with people in the field whose success I admired, whose record was proven, and whose counsel I regarded. I spoke with several dozen. One of those was Phyllis Allen, now vice president of Sharp Hospital in San Diego. She looked over the list quickly and passed it back to me. "There's something that's not here and it is probably the most important of all. It's integrity."

It took me by surprise. It was true, integrity wasn't on the list. I guess I felt it was a given, so integral a part of our work that I didn't even think of including it. I thought: I'll fix her. I'll not only add it, but I'll make it "impeccable integrity." Now that's a lot of integrity! To my surprise, and no surprise at all, it was considered the most important factor of every single person I interviewed. It also came out the highest of the most important qualities that were checked on the questionnaires I sent out (see appendix II). It was virtually everyone's most critical criterion.

When Phyllis Allen talked to me about integrity, she said: "If there is even the slightest feeling that we're not open and honest, we do ourselves and our institution a terrible disservice. We have to be exemplary. It's a matter of ethics. The donor's needs are first. We have to demonstrate an accountability. First of all and most important, we represent the institution and we have to represent it honestly and fairly, and people have to really feel and sense this. Integrity comes first. We have to conduct ourselves—personally and in work—above reproach."

If this is truly the most important factor, and it is, is it something that can be learned in later life? Should it be offered at seminars and workshops? Should it be the topic at major conferences? John Dolibois says: "We have never been successful in building character where it didn't already exist. A person either has integrity or he doesn't. I think we need to talk more about the single code of our profession rather than the craft."

Those who work in psychological behavior tell me that integrity is a characteristic which can be learned in later life, but only with the greatest transformation of soul and mind. For most, it is something instilled in early childhood by environment or an important influence. All of my great fundraisers benefited from this type of early motivation.

Principles may be inborn. Ethics, sometimes mandated. But integrity requires moral courage, magnetized by a fervor for an ideal. The complete fundraiser is a union of integrity, energy, and determination—the greatest of these is integrity. A man with integrity is a majority.

It permeates every aspect of a fundraiser's activity. It demands a singleness of purpose, purged of compromise. It means telling it as it is. Always. Tactfully. But firm. It means reflecting the highest principles. Always. A devotion to what is right and honest and just.

The measure of a great fundraiser is ultimately not recorded in meeting dollar objectives, building new facilities, or getting the large gift—although integrity actuates all of these. Integrity requires the stamina, the resourcefulness, and the daring of leadership. With it, a fundraiser can accomplish all things.

To reflect integrity is to invite trust. It commands respect. It demands total loyalty to the institution, a commitment to its cause and mission.

Morals. Ethics. Standards. Integrity. From these flow a torrent of values. Deeds, not words. It is a clear case of what you do and what you are that speak with such deafening impact— not what you say you are.

There is a price. And the price is always work, patience, and self-sacrifice. And a devotion to a supreme purpose. It can be a rigorous test. For an individual and an organization, integrity isn't a sometimes thing. It is everything.

The other day, I was having lunch with Mary Kay Ash. She is founder and inspiration behind the successful Mary Kay

Cosmetics. She is a beautiful person in every way and immensely generous—with her time, her talent, and her money. I was talking with her about what qualities she felt were essential for the fundraiser of one of the organizations where she is a trustee. She went through a number of talents that she felt were important and finally settled on one which she felt was most crucial of all—the ability to communicate. She went on.

"You know, at Mary Kay, we don't sell cosmetics."

I was shocked. "You don't?"

"No, we don't sell cosmetics. We sell—Hope!"

To Mary Kay, it is not only a matter of communicating, but doing it with drama and excitement. And it means understanding fully what you are trying to sell and how to package that boldly and effectively. When a person goes to a hardware store to buy a drill, he doesn't go to the store to buy a drill because he needs a drill. He buys a drill because he wants a hole! In fundraising, the ability to communicate means understanding that your prospects want the hole, and then making it so enticing it is irresistible.

Andre Heiniger, the former chairman of Rolex, was having dinner one evening when a friend of his stopped by the table to say hello. "How's the watch business?" "I have no idea," Heiniger replied. It seemed incredulous that the head of the world's most important watchmaker said that he didn't know what was going on in his own industry. But Heiniger was adamant. "Rolex is not in the watch business. We are in the business of luxury."

Federal Express emphasizes speed, dependability, and size. But what they are really selling is peace of mind. In fundraising, proper packaging, knowing what will motivate a prospect—that makes the real difference.

Lee Iacocca says that the ability to communicate is everything. Buck Smith says: "The ability to communicate is essential. It probably takes precedence over everything. Communication also implies empathy and sensitivity." And that is a key factor to keep in mind. It is not only important to be able to get your idea across, you must be empathetic. You must understand what it means to package effectively, to wrap your program in a magnificent gift box, tied with a beautiful ribbon.

I remember talking with Boone Powell when the architect came in with the plans for the new radiology department. Boone looked at them and said: "A donor won't be very interested in this space if it just says 'office.' Whose office is it? The department's director? Good, then let's write in Director's Office! That sounds better and will have more appeal if a donor thinks he's providing office space for someone at that level. You can make everything sound better and be more appealing if you use your imagination while being specific at the same time.

"Let's also make certain each piece of new equipment is fully described, and maybe we ought to consider putting the cost of the equipment where everybody can see it and understand what it's costing Baylor to furnish it. We may get someone who is grateful enough that they would be willing to make a gift for the equipment." Now Boone, he understands packaging!

Communications: Writing, speaking, listening. I'll deal with listening a little bit later—it's the one communication skill which is likely the most important and the least appreciated. But we all understand that the ability to motivate gifts at the highest level is in major part the ability to communicate.

A friend of Winston Churchill said that Churchill spent a good part of his life rehearsing his impromptu speeches. Mark Twain observed that the secret of a good impromptu speech is careful preparation. Jim Bowers pairs enthusiasm with communication. "In a way, enthusiasm and communication go hand in hand. Your enthusiasm for the institution is contagious. It is a tremendously important component of our work. I don't see how you can possibly sell a major gift unless you demonstrate enthusiasm for the need." This doesn't mean stretching. That gets back to the whole matter of integrity. And it certainly wasn't Thoreau's response when someone accused him of exaggerating. "Of course I exaggerate, it's the only possible way to come close to the truth."

The men and women I interviewed felt that skill in communicating was a given, you simply had to have it to be effective in the work. And this is important. Every single one felt that it is a talent one can learn. Beyond that, each indicated that you cannot only learn the skill, but you can understand how to motivate people effectively through your communications. The key element is that you have got to want this skill keenly enough that you are willing to really work to gain the competency. For some, that means really work! It may not come easily, but for all, it is something you can learn if you take the time and suffer the agony.

The people I consider to be the really inspired fundraisers are all impressive communicators. They know how to write and speak persuasively. That doesn't necessarily mean that they are creative writers. You can purchase excellent writing skills for a brochure or a folder. I mean something as simple as being able to write a good letter. In terms of verbal skills, it isn't necessarily the talent to speak to large groups that is important—although that is helpful. What is important is to have sufficient verbal skills that you can motivate a small group of people, or be persuasive one on one. This is really what counts.

Boone Powell said to me: "I think I'm a pretty fair fundraiser. The thing that keeps us in front of the pack at Baylor Medical Center is that we're always first in services, and we've been able to get the money to do it. Of every 20 developments, we're out front 19 times out of 20. We'll package something, put a story together, think about who should be given the opportunity to underwrite it, and then we give them the chance to be happy. That's what really happens when people make a gift—they're really happy to do it. They glow. It's just our job to communicate with them, give them the opportunity. And most of all, you have to keep it simple. It musn't be anything fancy. Most of the time, we just talk to our largest donors about a gift. No razzle-dazzle folders. We keep it simple." As Thoreau said: "Simplify, simplify, simplify. . . ." "Well," Boone Powell would ask, "why didn't he use just one 'simplify'?"

The great fundraisers I know are pretty fair writers, excellent editors, and have superior verbal skills. What sets them apart from the average and mediocre is their ability to listen.

Most of the great ones I spoke with told me that they really do not concentrate on getting a gift or asking for a donation. Instead, they spend their time talking about the vision and the dreams of the institution. Schuller told me that he did not seek money and gifts: "I am the communicator, the vehicle. I talk about our future and our destiny."

A fundraiser needs imagination first, then enthusiasm, and finally the ability to communicate. The greatest of these is communication, for without it, all else is lost. The art of persuasion means presenting information so provocatively, prospects will make up their own minds in favor of the program without being pushed. Aha, without feeling or knowing that they are being pushed! They will not realize that they have been motivated to do so.

One of the fundamental rules of fundraising is that to the degree that you give others what they want, they will give you what you want. It is the weightiest weapon in our fundraising arsenal. No other single factor is as important in motivating others to action.

Giving prospects what they want, that's what we are all about. That's how to get the gift. Persuading, leading, motivating, guiding, influencing—and listening.

Someone once said that persuasion is the art of telling someone to go to hell, and have them look forward to the journey! Persuasion is more likely to be just the ability to listen. Mary Kay Ash put her finger on it: "All through school we are taught to read, write, and speak. But we're never taught to listen."

Listening may be the most undervalued of all the communication skills, but good fundraisers consistently and committedly listen more than they speak. Abraham Lincoln said: "When I am getting ready to reason with a man and sell him on what concerns me, I spend one-third of my time thinking about myself and what I am going to say. Then I spend two-thirds thinking about him and about what he is going to say. Then, I just sit back, cross my legs, and listen. If I listen long enough and carefully enough, I will sell my program."

The trouble with most fundraisers is that they have too great a love for talking! One of the dictums of the Ford Motor Company is: "The salesman's job is not to sell a car. It is to assist the customer in buying a car. And to do this, you listen." To paraphrase something that Stanley Marcus, the genius behind the successful Neiman Marcus, said recently: "The greatest problem fundraisers face today is getting back to the important business of cultivating clients and understanding their institutions better. Too many are involved with long-range planning meetings. Or they are too busy playing golf, or attending conferences. One thing for certain, they aren't spending enough time listening to their customers and calling on them."

Mark well what Ernest Hemingway said. Note it carefully, every word. He was speaking to the fundraiser. "When people talk—listen. Listen completely. Don't be thinking what you're going to say. Most people never listen. Nor do they observe. You should be able to go into a room and when you come out, know everything that you saw there. And not only that, if the room gave any feeling, you should know exactly what it was that gave you the feeling. Practice listening. Practice observing. Practice." That quotation is worth a college credit course in fundraising.

The great fundraisers are not characterized by "the bird-of-prey" instinct which seems to motivate the average in the field. The truly outstanding fundraisers practice the art of letting the prospect sell himself. And there is only one way of doing that—by listening. If you do this effectively, you realize that "no," is no answer.

Mark H. McCormack speaks to fundraisers when he says that we control the timing of the sale, but we take our cue from the buyer—at least we do if we're smart. Obviously, this places a premium on listening rather than talking, on really hearing what the prospect is telling you rather than paying it "ear service." Tom Peters says that "listening is the winning approach. It is everything."

"Everyone, when they are young, has a little bit of genius; that is, they really do listen. They can listen and talk at the same time. When they grow a little older, many of them get tired and listen less and less. But some, very few, continue to listen. Those who listen most, learn most." Gertrude Stein was speaking to us.

All those I interviewed spoke about this invincible quality. Each one. Take Buck Smith, for instance. He says: "Fundraising is a listening job. That's what we are all about. Listening creatively and absorbing quickly. There is no way to qualify this or to put it in a formula. If you really want to reach people, you have to learn to listen. The trouble is, some people just never really learn this quality. In our profession, it is indispensable." Father Hesburgh said that you can't observe with your mouth open. I like that. He said that it is impossible to learn anything about the donor's wishes while you are talking. To motivate you really have to listen.

Brian Lurie agrees: "Listening is of extraordinary importance. If you can establish what really interests your prospect, you can get a large gift. But you can't find what interests them unless you really listen."

Albert Einstein applied a theory to it. He said that if A equals success, then the formula is: $A = X + Y + Z^2$. X stands for Work, Y for Play, and Z Learning to Listen. Brian Lurie is one with Einstein: "I believe to be an effective fundraiser you have to be alive. You have to love life. You have to have an effervescent quality. And most importantly, you have to be able to listen."

Most of the great ones actually find this part of their work the most fascinating and challenging. It's a riddle, encased in a puzzle: What does the prospect want most? The answer is critical to our success. What's going on inside the mind of the prospect? It's our responsibility to untangle the puzzle. And then to match their need with ours. This is the great secret.

If you let prospects ask enough questions—if you probe, search, encourage—you can find out what their interests are. In every session with a new person, the perceptive fundraisers spend most of their time finding out what is in the head and heart of the prospect. At least 95 percent of the initial interview is spent seeking and probing. Five percent is spent closing. You know if you have done a successful job of listening you will close the gift the very next time you are with the prospect. You listen for clues, subtle indications, little bits and pieces here and there that make the package more attractive to the prospects. You listen.

You have heard often about people who talk too much. You have never heard about anyone who listens too much!

Bruce Heilman agrees: "Listening," he said, "is important. Essential. Believe me, whenever I go out for a large gift, I listen. I listen very carefully. But then finally comes a time when you have to talk! Some people listen but never close. After you have done all of your careful listening, you must be able to motivate the prospect to a close." Listening and motivating—the greatest tools in fundraising.

"We can do all the research, and have the largest staff, and the most effective equipment, and the latest data and periodicals to do the research." John Miltner is stressing for me the importance of listening. "But the best facts come from the prospects. If we listen, we really can develop a strategy. Listening is actually a communication skill. We teach public speaking and elocution. What we really need to do is teach listening. It is one of the most important communication skills."

Boone Powell, Sr. is one of the great masters of listening. "You've got to hear people out. Almost all people have something they want to say. It's hard for a fundraiser, but you've got to listen rather than talk. That's true in almost any profession, but particularly so in fundraising. Even patients complain that doctors won't listen to them. I think what people want most in life is to have people listen to them. And if you listen carefully enough, you'll find out what the person is interested in giving to. You do your research, you know all about the person, and then you listen. I talked with this one person and listened very carefully. With enough prodding, I found out that he was really interested in research, especially if the research was first in its field. It just so happened that we had something at Baylor that we were working on at the time and I said to him: 'Knowing you as I do, this is going to really be down your alley.' He couldn't wait. 'Tell me, tell me—what is it? What kind of research are you talking about?'" Then Boone said to me: "I knew I had his attention! And it was not from talking, nothing eloquent I said. It was from listening."

Among churchpeople, I consider Dr. George Regas one of the great fundraisers of this quarter century. George is a Canon of the Episcopal Church, rector of All Saints in Pasadena, California—the largest Episcopal congregation west of the Mississippi River. I have watched him carefully when he calls on a prospect. Or rather, when he "listens on a prospect." He has a way of tilting his head to the side, gaining very close eye contact, and then becoming totally absorbed in what the prospect is saying. At that given time, nothing is more important to George Regas than what the person is saying. Now, I imagine a great deal of this comes from George's pastoral work. But not all clergy have this great talent for listening. To George Regas, it is an art form. He is sincerely interested. He is intent. He is captivated. And he always gets his gift.

Philip Hamburger tells the story how for many years he kept a tattered bulletin board in his kitchen, every inch covered with tacked-up addresses, memos, cards from loved ones, and quotations from Shakespeare and Yeats. Among all this debris was an old newspaper photograph of Franklin D. Roosevelt, leaning on a cane and listening intently to two ragged men who appear to have stopped him somewhere. Hamburger had no idea where the picture came from, but it was one of his priceless treasures. One of the men is small and scrappy-looking. His hands are in his pockets and he is leaning into Roosevelt's face. The other man, larger and older, is wearing an ancient gray coat, and is unshaved. Roosevelt's gray fedora is somewhat smashed, as was his custom. It's obvious from the photograph that Roosevelt is absolutely absorbed in everything the man is saying to him. He is attentive to every word. The caption reads: "He knew how to listen."

The problem is that many fundraisers can't stop talking. Too often they forget the basic rule of selling: Find out what the customer wants, and give it to them. To be effective in this business, you have got to "suspend your own agenda." You must forget what you were going to say and try to sell, and listen to what your prospect wants to say. General Electric has a saying: Give the customers more and more of what they want, and less and less of what they don't want. That should be written on one of those little yellow "Post-It" note sheets, and put on the draft of every proposal we prepare.

Jim Bowers says that he feels listening is one of the most understated qualities in our business, and often overlooked. "Fundraisers don't think about this very often but actually, listening is one of the most important factors in our business. It's a real talent. It's a skill that you can actually cultivate, but it takes some working. You have to really care enough to work at it. I don't know why more people don't give the kind of attention to listening that it deserves. In our business, it's crucial."

It comes in varying degrees, this ability and willingness to listen. The really great fundraisers all have it. Leaders in other fields have it to different levels. General George Patton, for instance, was an extraordinary strategist, an astute student of past wars and history, and an unflinchingly brave soldier. And he listened to no one! General George C. Marshall, a general and statesman without parallel, listened to everyone and heard everything. He missed nothing, sought advice and counsel of even the smallest detail. He made his associates and subordinates feel that every good idea was theirs. General Douglas MacArthur, on the other hand, had hearing that was totally selective. He listened to only those who told him what he wanted to hear. Even though he sought discussion, he never listened. His decisions were predetermined and he kept his own counsel. He pretty much did what he had already decided he would do, no matter where the discussion led. As Lincoln once told his cabinet: "I hear nine affirmatives and I vote nay. The nays have it!" His vote was the most equal of all. Practice listening and you are a winner. Do most of the talking and you motivate no one.

If listening is truly one of the major factors in successful fundraising—and it is—why aren't we teaching it? Unlike many of the other important skills, this is one that can be learned. Why aren't we offering it at any of our seminars or workshops? I was at a conference recently that covered, among others, these subjects: Writing a Case Statement, Development Software, Planned Giving Software, Successful Special Events, Employee Campaigns, and Marketing Planned Giving. Not one of these, not one, has anything to do with being a really successful fundraiser. Why aren't we teaching listening?

To be a good listener, you really have to work at it. The prospect must have confidence in you as an individual. You have to earn this. You convince them that you are truly interested in them and their concerns. You can't fake it. If you don't have a concern and a love for people, and you don't really believe in the mission of your institution—you won't be able to fake it. And you won't be convincing to them. To really listen, you share your ideas, and more importantly, you get the prospect to share his or her ideas. Find answers to their questions and their problems. Give the prospect a real opportunity to talk about what is on his or her mind. Avoid the fundraisers "bulldozer approach"—which covers a great deal of ground of glowing puffery and almost always results in not hitting the hot button you were looking for in the prospect.

The Spanish philosopher José Ortega said that he never thought that he would meet a man who was as interesting as an idea. But he listened, and he did! If you listen, you will find the man, and indeed, you will find his idea and his dream. If you listen carefully and intently, you will discover his passions. You will untangle every riddle, unlock every door. Listening gets the gift. Listening is the poetry of fundraising.

****

12 Vision Alone Gives Us Only a Visionary

It's . . . "like a dog walking on its hind legs. It is not done well, but you are surprised to find it done at all."
—Samuel Johnson

"Decide what it is you want to do, and then start doing it. At some point, you have got to do it!"
—Harold Geneen

"I had a certain talent, didn't I?"
—Beethoven's Last Words on His Deathbed

We had just completed a rigorous six hours. I had been interviewing Boone Powell, Sr. the whole day—interrupted at times with a senior staff person coming in to get advice, a telephone call or two with a major donor, and a quick tour of some very special new facilities at Baylor Medical Center. The tour took longer than it should have. We must have stopped a hundred times. There were warm handshakes for staff members, greetings for a dozen nurses, joking with physicians, a few times there was an exchange of a fishing adventure, and not less than a dozen hugs. This man is loved.

Near the end of the day, Boone looked at his watch, and said: "Do you want to have some fun, Jerry. Do you really want to have some great fun?"

I was exhausted. He is now 75 years old, but he never stops. He has had a couple of hip operations and he must have been a wild terror when he was in true racing form! I wasn't ready for "fun," but I figured that Boone is a Baptist, and what the heck! What kind of serious fun could a Baptist get in to? "Sure, Boone—let's have some fun."

He grabbed my arm and we headed for the patient rooms. We spent the next hour visiting patients. That was Boone's idea of having fun.

Boone Powell has served over 40 years at Baylor University Medical Center in Dallas. And every year has been a celebration. He is Baylor Medical Center!

Baylor is the second largest not-for-profit hospital in the country. The largest is the Baptist Hospital in Memphis—and the administrator there is Boone's brother. Boone is no longer administrator at the hospital. He was succeded by his son, one of the most effective administrators and most respected spokesmen in the business. The apple doesn't fall far from the tree!

Although he claims that "I am just an old country boy," Boone, Sr. was the driving force, the strategist, the dynamo that took a small hospital and made it one of the largest and most distinguished health care institutions in the nation. He has received every major honor it is possible to bestow on a hospital administrator and also served as president of the national group.

He says that most hospitals haven't explored the potential in their own backyard. "You can go around the world looking for money or bemoaning the fact that you don't have enough in your own community. I was very much influenced in my youth by a speech called 'Acres of Diamonds.' I think most people would find that they have acres of diamonds in their own backyard." He says that all he really wants to do in life is to go fishing but he carries the title of consultant at the medical center and his presence continues to be felt. Just like George Burns, he is too old to retire.

When Boone puts on that "country boy routine," I keep my hands in my pockets! You know you're going to end up giving a gift. A big gift.

He was born in Etowah, Tennessee. He went to North Georgia College, which had a student body of 300. He has strong church background and has always been active. He is alive and vital. A perpetual youth. Those bad hips don't seem to slow him down and he never talks about them. He is the embodiment of what Frank Lloyd Wright meant when he said:

"Death is something you can do nothing about, nothing at all. But youth is a quality and if you have it, you never lose it."

Boone has never lost his sparkle. His mental arteries haven't hardened either. He is crystal sharp. Though average in stature, he has immense presence. And it's heart that counts—his is larger than Texas is wide.

He has raised over $200 million for Baylor University Medical Center. He passes that off with a wave of the hand. He says he hasn't been personally responsible and that he didn't do it alone. Wait a moment—he has been personally responsible! Yes, he did have help—he empowered it.

One of the latest and newest dandies of management style is the "walking around" concept. Boone Powell has been doing that for more than 40 years and didn't even know that he was practicing good management! "I know a lot of administrators that never get out of their office. I just don't see how they can manage the operation that way. I love to walk the halls. I love to get in to patient rooms and to talk with patients. I love to visit with the staff and the doctors. I hear a lot of people saying that philanthropy is dead. Philanthropy isn't dead, they are."

If there was any single message at all in Tom Peters' *In Search of Excellence* it was—stay close to your customers, wander around. There's no real magic to it, no mumbo-jumbo. Just stay as close as you possibly can to your prospects, and keep in close enough contact that you know how they are feeling. What they are feeling. What is necessary to make them buy. You don't need market research and you don't need demographic information. Just stay close.

Stay close! I don't know if the story is apocryphal but it was told to me by someone at Ochsner Clinic who should know, and it does sound to me like classic Boone Powell. Some time ago, one of Baylor's important friends and largest donors had to have a special operation which could best be performed at Ochsner. Boone made all of the arrangements for the operation, contacted the specific physician who would be leading the team for the operation, and even arranged for a special room. Every-thing was in perfect order. It took about a half dozen telephone calls or so, followed by as many letters—but I suppose any administrator would do that for an important friend. But there was more. On the day the man entered Ochsner for admission, he was accompanied by Boone. Powell made the trip with him from Dallas to New Orleans—walked him through the admissions process, and went with him to his room. And now, dear readers, that's the epitome of "staying close." I didn't find out the end of that story, but I'd guess (Baptists don't bet!) that Baylor got the next gift, not Ochsner.

He sees dollar signs. He has a brilliant mind that darts, dips, and swoops with terrifying speed and penetrating accuracy. A dozen ideas a minute. For him, each contact for a major gift becomes the stage on which he acts out a drama. But here's the important point, and it must not be missed. Boone Powell, Sr. loves people. It is what drives him on. He firmly believes that he is saving lives. Each contact stirs his soul. Inspires him to be his very best. For some who don't know him, it appears he is practicing all the wiles of witchcraft. It is indeed, pure magic. A magic performed out of his great compassion and love for people.

Is all of this a role for the administrator? He says: "There's no substitute for the CEO making calls—regardless of the institution. I know at Baylor, a patient is so impressed when I come walking in the room. It's not me, it's the fact that I was the chief officer."

He is a ten speed bicycle racer in a three speed world. He has extraordinary capacity which comes out of his great devotion to the institution and his love of people. He kept talking to me about the joy people get in giving. Joy—he used the term dozens of times in our dicussion. He is not asking for a gift. He is simply giving people an opportunity to experience exhilarating joy. "When I talk to someone about our program, I never think about getting a gift. Fundraising is nothing more than spreading joy." All of the great ones spoke about this phenomenon—to them, it wasn't work, it was fun, and they were just helping people to experience joy.

Effective fundraisers must bring to their job sufficient skill. They must be able to accomplish or oversee the mechanics of the job. But what counts most is the human skill in working and motivating prospects and volunteers. To be successful, you build a cooperative effort. And there must be conceptual skills, sufficiently so that you recognize the interrelationships of all of the factors involved in each situation. This is what leads to proper action and achieves optimum good for the total organization.

Vartan Gregorian says that one of his great strengths is that he connects things. By that he means he is able to go from one concept to another and see how all are irreversibly wed.

Many fail in our business because they cannot join the beginning with the end. Warren Bennis says that somehow the leader must find time to deal with the important and the non-routine. In his book *Why Leaders Can't Lead*, Bennis says: "The leader, at every level, must be partly a conceptualist, something more than just an idea man. By that I mean someone with a kind of entrepreneurial vision, a sense of perspective, and most of all the time spent thinking about the forces that will affect the destiny of that person's shop or institution." But that takes time, thinking, planning. Being able to stop and set yourself apart from the tedious and the minutia—and as Gregorian says, connect things.

Planning is the key. Bruce Heilman says: "You can't do anything well without the proper planning. If you plan what you want to accomplish, how you are going to get there, and how you are going to get the money—then you are going to get there. You can't do it without planning. At the University of Richmond, we made a decision as to where we wanted to be, and how we wanted to get there. Our careful planning increased the excitement that was necessary for raising the money." But how do you take time for the thinking and planning when you are up to your kazoo in alligators and telephone calls you haven't returned? Euripides warns us that we must not slight what is near even though we are aiming at what is far.

One of the marks of a great fundraiser is the ability to respond instantly to a query, to say precisely the proper thing under moments of great stress. To speak in words that never offend. Although we at times do! To follow all proffered advice. Although at times, we do not! We fundraisers face more than our share of spontaneous situations. No matter what extraordinary strategy you plan, no matter what great design you conceive, you may be certain that the unexpected and the trivial will disrupt your plans.

You have to know where you are going. An old Turkish proverb says if you don't know where you are going, any road will get you there. "Vision alone gives us only a visionary." That's Father Hesburgh speaking. He doesn't mean that in a pejorative sense. He says that you have to join vision with faith, and when you do—mountains begin to move.

In this business, it never ends. There are always mountains to move. It requires commitment, conviction, and will of steel. We have all seen some in the business who intend to take a definite stand in the middle of what appears to be a muddle. They will not succeed. Of Howard Taft, the 27th president, Theodore Roosevelt said: "He means well, but means well feebly."

All of the men and women I interviewed are big-picture people. They conceptualize. It's mostly instinct. They sense when ideas are in collision and know intuitively when important pieces are fitting together. They are "the forest people." Then there are the "tree people." The latter are the lesser fundraisers. They get great joy in digging into all of the detail and complexity of a puzzling prospect, so much so that it absorbs all of their intellectual and physical energy. They don't have the time nor the disposition to go after the prospect or even to sit back and reflect on the implication of all of the facts.

The most successful fundraiser is one who can conceptualize, who as Mary Parker Follet puts it: "One who sees another picture not yet actualized. He sees the things which belong to the present but which are not yet there. And then finally, to the prospects, he makes certain that they feel it is not his purpose or the organization's which is to be achieved, but a common purpose, born of the desires and the needs of the community and to serve a higher cause."

Robert L. Katz heads a consulting firm specializing in corporate strategy and is a director of a number of publicly held corporations. Katz says that he is not sanguine about the degree to which conceptualizing can be developed. "A lesser person has learned to think this way early in life, it is unrealistic to expect a major change on reaching executive status." He indicates that changing jobs, special interdepartmental assignments, and working with specific problems can certainly provide opportunities for a person to enhance previously developed conceptual abilities. "But I question how easily this way of thinking can be incalculated after a person passes adolescence. In this sense, then, conceptual skills should perhaps be viewed as an innate ability."

This attribute is of crucial importance. There appears to be evidence that it is innate. But it can be learned, honed, molded. It will require great effort, a commitment to its importance, and a willingness to strive. At the lower levels in our field, it is possible that our greatest need is for technical skills and, of course, superb human relations. At higher levels, technical skills become relatively less important. They are superseded with the need for conceptual and strategic skill, and this increases in geometric proportions.

The ability to conceptualize did not receive the highest ratings, but it was consistently mentioned by all. E.B. White said that he saw a great future for complexity! To have great visions for your organization, the high expectations, the bold plans—this distinguishes the great ones. They look to the years ahead as the time of their greatest achievement.

Conceptual skill means recognizing how all of the functions of the organization are interrelated and intertwined, and how one depends on the other. It means understanding how changes in one part affect all the others. Most of all, it extends to visualizing the relationship of all of the institution's constituencies. If we do not take the responsibility for changing our direction, we are likely to end up where we are headed.

I know one major hospital in the southeast which has enjoyed great success over the years. But the environment in healthcare today is a jungle, and in recent years the hospital has not done well. Its marketing is misdirected, its mission dulled, and its planning flawed. This hospital is like some people—packed in an automobile driven by a child traveling downhill at a blinding speed, without brakes. The sign posts all along the way are marked "progress." But it is on a collision course.

The Chinese have a saying that "The situation is totally impossible . . . but not serious." For the great fundraiser, the road ahead is always lined with opportunities and immense potential. To reach for your own summit, you must visualize success and empower men and women to have the joy in investing and sharing with you in the magic of the adventure.

Some of you have worked in institutions or for people who practice the N.I.H. Syndrome—Not Invented Here. It's like "a wall of molasses." You can't get anything in. You can't get anything out. You're stuck. But we all understand that great things can be achieved if we don't care who gets the credit.

The great fundraisers spoke about the power, the immense inspiration of an idea. They understand, also, that these powerful dreams and ideas do not float around in never-never land. For an idea to come to fruition, it must be magic. You engage a prospective donor, you grab him by the lapels and shake him. It is a strike of lightning.

Often, important ideas come modestly and silently. The great fundraisers are idea people. Not faint of heart, often not even tidy-minded. But they possess a resilient spirit which knows no limit. They recognize there are no easy victories. No easy solutions. But they all have a driving passion for solving problems. They understand that new ideas are the life-line of their organization—that's what gets the large gift.

The world is filled with critics, cranks, and curmudgeons. New ideas are often met with an extraordinary lack of action and a digging in of the heels. The spirit which welcomes non-conformity is fragile indeed.

We fundraisers live in a time of change. Unbelievable, indescribable, and unpredictable change. The self-satisfied and complacent will not survive. What is good enough today will be out of date tomorrow. The successful fundraiser never feels he has arrived. Never feels comfortable. Knows that today's solutions are simply not good enough for tomorrow. Understands that his tasks are never completed. Acts instead of reacts. Never waits for things to happen. Gives up the old and seeks the new. Has an unrelenting "can do" attitude in everything. Innovation is the key.

It means creating a new twist, an imaginative turn. Daring new concepts and exciting new ideas. The successful fundraiser is receptive, curious, unafraid, and willing to try anything. He zests for the unexplored and is committed to a better way. Experimentation and exploration, always seeking new approaches to solve problems.

And here is the secret. The genius of the successful fundraiser is to see the relationship between philosophy, programs, and ideas—even though they may seem unrelated. And then combine them into some new form, some new and bold concept. It's the Vartan Gregorian dictum: to connect the seemingly unconnected, to perceive what others have seen, and to create what no one else has thought to attempt.

The world is filled with lackluster mediocrity. The future belongs to those who develop an innovative approach. New methods, new combinations, new applications. These are the sparks which will ignite a blaze. You must recognize that to say "impossible" always puts you on the losing side.

You have come to that moment. You have done the proper research. Everything seems in order. You have made all the connections. You understand the needs of the prospect, you sense what propels him. The project is a perfect fit. The packaging is superb and now you must inspire action. It takes motivational genius.

Bruce Heilman says: "You must encourage and inspire. You have got to motivate prospects to be the best they can be. You have got to really feel you are giving them the opportunity to do something special. To save lives or change lives. I've never felt that I am a money raiser. I am a missionary for a cause. And that's what inspires action." George Engdahl says that it comes from really believing in what you are doing and demonstrating your dedication to the program. That's contagious, and it inspires action.

Milton Murray told me that it only happens when people have dreams. "They have visions. A fundraiser must act and he has to know how to motivate others into action. If you can't do that, you'll never really be effective at fundraising." You may know computer software from A to Z, you may understand psychodemographics and how it relates to a direct response program, you may have perfect office procedure and an office manual which is detailed and explicit—but if you can't inspire a donor to make a gift, it is without meaning.

****

13   Playing a Poor Hand Well

"I have always known that writing is indecent exposure. By publishing a book, one asks to be attacked."

—Peter F. Drucker

"Words! Words! Words!"

—Eliza Doolittle, from My Fair Lady

"Very dangerous things, theories."

—Dorothy Sayers

Louis Pasteur's contributions were of incalculable value.

He was able to halt an epidemic of cholera, at the time the scourge of the world; innoculate a boy for hydrophobia; discover the etiology of anthrax and develop a vaccine for it; prove convincingly that yeasts ferment beer; discover how to preserve wine; isolate the bacillus in a disease that destroyed silkworms; discover how to rid milk of its life's threatening disease. And much more, dozens of extraordinary achievements.

Toward the end of his life, he said to a friend: "How beautiful! And to think that I did it all!" It was a moment of both modest astonishment and pride. He had done it all. In his extraordinary and enviable life, it was his privilege to achieve the unachievable.

We fundraisers, how fortunate we are. We too have the opportunity to save lives. To achieve the unachievable. Our days are full, alive with auspicious moments. But at times our emphasis is almost entirely focused on getting the gift. Reaching the budget. Putting the campaign over. These, of course, are essential to our work. It does, after all, represent our personal report card!

Too often, however, we get so wrapped up in these score cards—our bottom line—we lose sight of why we are really in this business, our true objective—to change lives and to save lives. Pasteur through science, we through fundraising. We are at it every day, raising funds to build our new cancer center. Cure diabetes. Send a kid to camp or college. Support the symphony. Furnish guide-dogs. We are one with Pasteur: At the end of our career we, too, can say: "How beautiful! And to think that I did it all!"

When I write about the great fundraisers, I refer entirely to those on the firing line, those who set their sights and souls on seeking the gift. The exhilarating one-on-one contest that takes place between the caller and the prospect.

Complex and puzzling, these times. Fundraising is no different. There is cause-related fundraising, telemarketing, scientific response-mailing, the new life insurance, and donor analysis by demographics and psychodemographics. It's all very exciting and productive. And of critical consequence to our organizations. But I refer to that as raising funds and make my distinction with that and fundraising. I have no quarrel with the former, although I am certain I show my bias. I have chosen, however, to write only about those characteristics and skills that are required to seek a gift, especially a large gift. I have established these limits without agony or apology.

How can you possibly explain the fact that virtually all of my great leaders were born or raised in small communities? This amazing fluke is . . . well, it's spooky!

Just look at this appealing bit of Americana—and this is only a sampling of where my great ones were born: Beaver Falls, Pennsylvania. Bell-Buckle, Tennessee. Gunn City, Missouri. Etowah, Tennessee. Conneaut, Ohio. Bad Axe, Michigan. El Dorado, Oklahoma. Buffalo, Minnesota. Jefferson City, Tennessee. Paw Paw, West Virginia. Newton, Mississippi. It poses a formidable question. Why? Is it of any significance, or is it sheer coincidence?

My great ones come from small colleges and small towns. And how do you explain the fact that in the current listing of men and women in *Who's Who in America,* 78 percent were born in communities of fewer than 25,000 people.

A definite and ever-present *ethos* appears to exist in a small town that promotes success among its young people. As Jim Bowers put it: "It seemed that everyone in Beaver Falls placed a very high priority on good education. Just about all the families of the kids I knew gave high importance to hard work and good grades. All of us were expected to go on to college. There was never any question about it. And we were expected to do well and take on important work." Rabbi Brian Lurie was one of the exceptions to the small town phenomenon. He was born in Cleveland, Ohio, but he understands the ethics which exist in small towns. "There is more of a sense of community. People in small towns have more control over their lives. The pace is different. And they are naive (and I mean this in the best sense) in their belief of a better world. They still have the wonderful American dream."

A recent study by the Episcopal church found that as families moved from smaller communities to major cities, their involvement in the church decreased. Further, as they moved from east to west in the country, their involvement decreased markedly. And the further west, the more it decreased. But there's more to the study, something quite strange. As they moved from single-family homes to apartments, involvement decreased even further. But wait, there's still one more point, even more bewildering. The higher the floor the apartment was on, the less their relationship to the church.

I'm not really certain how to provide scientific proof for this small town phenomenon. In a case which dealt with due process, Supreme Court Justice John Paul Stevens said: "I can't define obscenity, but I know it when I see it." To which Melvin Bell replied: "Bullshit. If you can't define it, you don't know what it is." Well, I can't define it!

But it's there, it exists, it's a matter of record. Let all those from Detroit and Buffalo, and those from large state universities, and those with no church background—let them all rise in protest!

Another coincidence is that almost all of my great fund-raisers received their undergraduate degrees from colleges of 2500 students or fewer. In the case of most, much fewer! This is perhaps an accident of my subjective selection of candidates to interview. Or perhaps the age of the men and women—they were older than the average of those in the field. Or possibly a result of the background of my people—that because they came from a small community and there was an important influence of the church, they chose a small college. Or maybe—no accident at all!

What if—well, what if there is something very special about the environment or the education provided at a small college that somehow enhances the qualities and skills necessary in becoming a great fundraiser?

Or take, for instance, the case of a small college in another discipline. Phillip Moffitt says that in the great race for engineers, MIT proves to be virtually a backwater institution, the sticks, when it comes to the most advanced form of engineering—solid-state electronics. Some contend that Grinnell College in Iowa, with its 1000 students, has been years ahead of MIT. The picture is the same in other great frontiers of technology in the second half of the 20th century.

My own evidence and data to the contrary, it is difficult for me to believe that a man or woman attending a large university would have any problem at all enjoying an extremely successful career in fundraising. I am equally confident that there is likely no relationship between the academic pursuit and the person's effectiveness as a fundraiser. The great ones seem to come from all sorts of educational backgrounds and disciplines.

If I were talking with a young person about going into our field, I would strongly recommend a well balanced liberal arts degree in the finest school possible, preferably a small one with good credentials in which a close relationship with the faculty is encouraged. I would also suggest one with a strong association with a church. That just happened to be my own bias, completely unsubstantiated by any sort of research, empirical or otherwise. And I would recommend lots of classes in philosophy, psychology, sociology, communications—especially public speaking—and English.

I was in Australia recently speaking to 400 vital men and women, all involved in fundraising in Australia and New Zealand. They are an extremely exciting group to be around, charged with energy. Fundraising is still sufficiently young in the southern hemisphere that there continues to be awe and wonder about the profession. These folks have high expectations, eager to the bone to succeed.

During one of our sessions, a leader in the group said that he hoped some day they would be offering a degree in fundraising from one of the Australian universities. I shuddered! I sincerely hope that will never happen. Imagine four years of filling men and women with the technique of fundraising, the mechanics, the routine, the rules and hoary verities. There would probably even be a course on computers!

I am convinced now that the means and methods of this business have very little to do with its success. It is the art of fundraising that really counts.

I am not at all certain that the art can best be taught on a campus or that it can be taught at all. From what I can best determine, the art is not taught, it is caught—and at a very early age.

There is more. I'll stand challenged for heresy on this one! I am convinced now that experience is very likely not an important success factor. Virtually all I interviewed agreed with me on this point.

When I talked with Buck Smith, he told me: "When I interview a person for a new fundraising job, I never worry too much about experience. If they have the characteristics that are necessary, I'm willing to take a chance. When you make a mistake with a person, it is usually because you've overlooked

the traits and characteristics which are essential. This sometimes gets overlooked because of a person's long experience in
the field—but I honestly think that the number of years in the
business is not relevant."

I am consulting at a university with a deeply important and
abiding relationship to its founding church. As part of our
work, I am helping it conduct a search for a development officer
for their College of Public Health. Because of the church's
dominance and emphasis in public health, we felt that the man
or woman should be selected from the membership of this
denomination. That was a given, no other choice was possible.

The university and the College of Public Health developed
a short list of candidates from this group. The interviewing
process began and it became obvious quite early that we were
in trouble!

"The problem is," said the dean, "our base is so terribly
narrow. We simply don't have many people from the church
who are in fundraising."

I told him to forget about finding someone with experience. I felt it was possibly the least important factor to consider in their situation. "Let's look for someone with all of the
qualities and skills that we need in this job. Perhaps there is
someone at the university who is doing something else entirely
different in some other field. Let's consider a professor, someone from the admissions staff, or in public relations, or a
secretary. Or let's look over our church membership in this area
and talk with some of our ministers. The important thing is,
let's look for a man or woman with the qualities we seek, and
not worry about the experience."

I know we'll find the person we need, precisely the right
person. He or she will bring the skills, talents, characteristics
and attributes we need for this particular position. The art of
fundraising, it will all be there—just below the surface ready to
be encouraged and stimulated. What we shall need to teach this
person are the techniques of fundraising—and that's the easiest
part of the business.

In one Catholic hospital in Florida, we recommended that the medical director be hired as the executive of their new foundation. Yes, a doctor! I was certain that he would be imminently successful in this position. He felt it was time to give up his active practice. For years he has been involved in one fundraising campaign or another for the hospital. He had all of the necessary attributes one would look for in this position. And of immense importance, even though he was of the Jewish faith, he loved the sisters and was totally dedicated to the mission of the hospital. It wasn't really an unusual choice at all. He was a natural.

You know them and so do I. Men and women with 15 or 20 years of experience in fundraising—but it's the same experience, repeated each year. Nothing new, nothing changed. The same drab, dreary person they have been for all those years. With the same drab, dreary approach.

Experience is not unimportant—but it's not important. Do you understand the distinction I make? Experience was not mentioned in a single interview as being significant. It was not mentioned once in the nearly 3,000 questionnaires returned to me. In my 30 years of consulting work, it has not been mentioned at all as being of consequence. Except, of course, by search committees that always seem to be looking for people "with the right kind of experience"—whatever that means.

Yes, yes, I know. Combine experience with all of the important talents and attributes—and you have a certain winner. You can bet on it. You can take it to the bank. You simply can't lose. But I assure you, also, that if you follow my design and go after men and women who have the proper skills and characteristics, you can make them into great fundraisers— even if they don't have the experience. In some cases, they can be great in spite of the experience they have had!

Stanford University recently announced its campaign for $1,000,000,000. That's a lot of zeros! It's the largest fundraising program ever undertaken in the history of whatever.

You'd expect the university to look for a man or woman who could bring to the fundraising role the greatest number of years of proven experience in the field. But that's not what they did. They chose Henry Riggs—a bright professor from the College of Engineering, who they named vice president for fundraising for the university.

Riggs had no prior experience in the field. What he did have were the necessary attributes that make a great fundraiser. And the innate skills that can turn a probable success into a certain winner. There's one thing more. Riggs brought an unrelenting devotion and commitment to the university. On every count, he fit the bill.

For those who are inclined to keep score on this sort of thing and are interested in checking on the welfare of the inexperienced Riggs—the campaign has not yet been officially announced, but they have over half of their money already reported. Those close to the situation say it is certain to be successful.

Notre Dame chose Bill Sexton, a professor from its School of Management to head its fundraising program. No prior experience. And the University of California, Berkeley selected a professor of botany to take over its development program and capital campaign. No prior experience. What's happening? What's going on?

Can anyone who brings to the table the appropriate qualities, skills, and characteristics—can he or she become an effective fundraiser? Experienced or not? Yes!

Can a successful IBM salesperson who brings the proper skills, talents, and characteristics—can he be successful in fundraising? Yes!

An attorney? Yes! A life insurance salesperson? Yes! An undertaker? Yes! You heard me, yes! A minister? Yes! Anyone. The key is having the right skills, talents, and attributes for the job.

The essence of the matter is in determining which of the essential criteria are needed for the job—and this will be described specifically and in detail in the next chapter.

All I interviewed agreed that the traits that make a successful fundraiser are transferrable and that someone from outside the field can do extremely well in fundraising if they met the criteria. At the same time, those who are successful in fundraising could be equally effective in another field. Bruce Heilman said that without question the qualities are transferrable. "I think that there are some factors that fundraisers enjoy to the same extent as a leader in almost any other field. You've got to be concerned about people, really concerned. And have high energy, and an ability to motivate. Being a good listener is essential, and then you have to inspire people to action. On top of that, all of the communication skills are important. These are all essential factors and I can't imagine that anyone can really win at this business without having them in equal amounts. A really successful fundraiser would probably be just as successful in almost any other field he attempted."

Jim Bowers said: "When I hire someone, I look for the qualities which make a person successful, and I tend to minimize the years of experience. A track record is important, not the number of years. But it may not necessarily be a track record in fundraising. It is entirely possible that they might have great success in another field where all of the important qualities are present and can be transferred. I think that anyone who is successful in his field will have these traits."

Those I interviewed were consistent in their comments regarding this matter. They feel that the qualities that are really important in fundraising are the same characteristics they see in leaders in every field. The great industrial leaders and financial leaders would have found their way to the top in fundraising, also. They feel just as strongly that the best fundraisers would be just as effective in the for-profit arena.

Related to all of this is the question of whether the man or woman makes the institution, or the institution makes the man or woman. Can the extraordinary fundraiser, the great professional, raise funds in even a dismal situation? Or does a distinguished organization with a very wealthy constituency—does it make the great fundraiser? Maurice Friedman says that no two men are ever in the same situation. Each brings a unique body-mind-spirit totality to his work and his decisions about life's values. And his organization, his work, his position, and his environment—they all mold him.

When Father Hesburgh went to Notre Dame, it was a small midwestern school, virtually unknown, and of no particular distinction. When Boone Powell became administrator at Baylor, it was a small hospital—good, but of no special merit. When W.A. Criswell went to Baptist in Dallas, it was a fine church, but nowhere near the size and super strength it is today. All of these people built their institution, molded it virtually out of clay into the type of image they wanted most.

Among all, however, there was the strong opinion, virtually unanimous, that the institution does make the man. They feel there are those institutions and organizations where it is virtually impossible not to succeed.

And of some organizations the cards are stacked against you—even for the best in our business. John Miltner was typical of those I spoke with. "I think that some institutions are such that they will continue to be successful and raise a lot of money, no matter who's on the job. And there are places where no matter how good you are, you simply couldn't do an effective job." George Engdahl agrees: "I believe that a strong institution makes a strong fundraiser. I honestly believe that some of the great institutions and organizations would do well with even average fundraiser. But given the strong institution and a strong fundraiser both, you could accomplish really great things."

It would certainly be much easier to sell a New York Philharmonic, a Stanford University, a National Gallery, a Mayo Clinic. In some organizations, it comes over the transom and under the doors! People like giving to a really successful and distinguished institution. Donors understand and demand excellence.

It has to be "the right" situation. There has to be the potential. There has to exist the constituencies with the proper resources.

It is an interesting question to explore—could my great ones, could they make it in a really difficult situation? Almost all of them did!

Bruce Heilman saved a condemned university. Buck Smith saved Chapman College from bankruptcy. Vartan Gregorian rescued the gasping New York Public Library. Schuller started with nothing.

If there is any potential at all, these great ones can pull it off. Where the magic will not work, is where the institution has a poor reputation and is not highly regarded—and wishes to do nothing about it. Or where the major constituencies simply don't have the resources for providing funds.

You can't raise money where it doesn't exist and you can't raise money for an organization that is unwilling to make a commitment to greatness. Even in those situations where it appeared that a rabbit was pulled out of the hat, these great fundraisers were able to perform their magic only when the organization was committed to doing something about the situation.

Innate or learnable? Achievable by anyone? This is the overriding question which gives substances and soul to my work and research. I think that the proof is conclusive.

At times you must wonder whether you have reached your full potential and when you say to yourself, as one says when dealt a poor hand in bridge, "I'll play with what I've got." An old casino axiom states that success in life comes not from holding a good hand, but in playing a poor hand well.

Knowing all of the techniques, mastering them—that can make a good fundraiser. But that's the science of our business. Having the proper characteristics and attributes, and plying these—that's the art of fundraising. And that's what the great ones are all about. The problem is that most of the factors that matter significantly in the art of fundraising are the most diffi-cult to explain. This is true of all art forms.

Let's talk about it, this art of fundraising. It is not unlike a painting and the artist. It is best accomplished by feel, instinct, some anguish, sensitivity, and a great deal of passion. Not by rules. To be certain, one must have an understanding of brush strokes, composition, balance, and the ingenious combining of colors. But these are regimented. The really great artist is inspired.

In spite of the many conferences, the myriad seminars, the ubiquitous workshops, little evidence remains that one can simply annoint people as really effective fundraisers. Someone once asked a well known midwest college president if there was such a thing as "a natural" fundraiser. "Yes," he said, "but no one starts out that way!"

We all want to be the best we possibly can be. We want to be great—for our organizations and for ourselves. We know we can't do this on a smile, wearing a power ensemble, or having the right handshake. Fundraising is less a science of mechanics and organizational structure than it is the art of persuasion and motivation. Some concentrate on the "how" of fundraising, but that's the science. The real winners focus on the "why"—and that is the art of this business.

The reality is that fundraising is more than just science and art. It is a puzzling, challenging contest. Or rather, perhaps, it is the sublime professional collage of all three.

If you take a wasp and feed it only royal honey, no matter how long you do this, it will not become a queen-bee. Can someone really change? Can we advance from what we are to be something exceptional and extraordinary? Plato said: "Know thyself." Nietzsche, "To be what thou art." Kierkegaard, "To be the self one truly is." To be yourself, and to be something quite special—how does this great transformation take place?

It's a continuing debate, with no definitive answers. Are

leaders born or made? Some feel the great leaders have been empowered with some genetic endowment of mystical proportions. For these people, somehow their destiny as a leader has been preordained. The truth is many major skills and competencies can be learned. Many factors on the list I shall discuss in the next chapter fall into this category. We are all educable. But it takes something special—it requires an immense desire and hunger, a compelling drive, to succeed. To be the very best.

The term "self-actualization" is used by behavioral scientists to express the idea that each of us has the potential for professional development. It is quite clear, however, that each of us grows to a greater or lesser degree, depending on our own drive. What self-actualization means, in terms of behavior, is that each of us makes a commitment to use his gifts as best he can and take advantage of every opportunity.

Learned or taught, it is quite clear that the great fundraisers are not "made" overnight. Nor are they simply "born." It is almost certainly a happy combination of the two.

Some subscribe to the "Great Man" theory—that greatness is vested in only a few select men and women. Some are born to lead, others must be led. Either you have it, or you do not. No amount of learning or yearning can change your fate. Few would buy that concept in total. But being a great fundraiser cannot be conferred. It must be earned. Many of the important talents and skills can be learned, but only with a rigorous and vigorous complete commitment to become all you can be. You must make a personal decision. You must do more than just wish it or want it. You must will it. And then take the responsibility for making it happen.

Talent is a rare gift. Competency is not. Competence is something one works at. Talent is another thing. It is essential for success in our work. And success takes talent plus dedication and complete commitment.

For many of the factors, the news isn't entirely good. It is clear that there are a number that are innate, inherent, over which you have virtually no control. There are many more that are shaped and formed during early childhood—probably by age 12 or 15.

Some attributes and characteristics, however, can be changed—but only if you determine it is sufficiently important to your career, and you are willing to undertake an excruciating transformation. A metamorphosis. Not all will wish to go through the agony. I can understand that. It may not be worth it for you. But to become great in this field, it will be essential.

The men and women I interviewed are on my side in this issue. "You can sharpen your skills with proper work and training, but the really great fundraisers have natural talent—and I'm not certain you can learn this." Buck Smith said that. Anita Rook says that you unquestionably bring innate talent to fundraising. "I don't think everyone is made to be a fundraiser. Much of what is important you are born with and there's not much you can do about that. But with the right kind of education and training, and if you really work at it, you can become very good in this field."

"What you see is what you get," says Milton Murray. "I don't think that you change people very much. If a person does not have certain skills, talents, or attributes, I don't think, there is much that you can do to change them. I used to think that I could change people but I am convinced now that this is an extremeley difficult task."

Boone Powell and I had a lengthy discussion on this topic. I felt that if anyone would have some sensitivity to the question, he should. During his long administration, he employed over 6,000 men and women at any given time—covering a wide range of skills and educational backgrounds. He looked over my list quite carefully, took time to review each single item. "You can't do much about teaching these principles. For instance, you either like people or you don't. You can't get that from a book. You've got to really love people in this business. I don't think you can read a book or go to school to learn how to be a fundraiser. You've got to have a feeling and a sensitivity for the work.

"You've got to be able to see the big scene in order to be good at this business. I don't think this can be taught. In fundraising, we have to impress upon our professionals the importance of these attributes, but they've really got to want to do the job. Some of the communication skills can be taught. But much of what makes a great fundraiser comes from the deep-seated feelings a person has. They're felt deep down. And if you don't have them, you can't learn them.

"Changing people is a very hard thing to do. I think that once you leave high school, you're really pretty well set. The mold is made and extremely difficult to change or break."

Dr. George Sheehan would be one who would say that a dramatic change might not always be desirable. "I don't drink much anymore. I'm never the life of any party. The hostess who invites me knows within the first five minutes she has made a mistake. I usually wander into the kitchen for a cup of coffee and then find a large book and a quiet place to read until the festivities are over. I have found out who I am and I have no intention of impersonating anyone else. Some people liked me better when I was drinking!"

The best of the fundraisers are naturals. There's no great magic to it. Common sense, ability to communicate easily, the talent to motivate people, a good memory and vocabulary, and a quick and analytical ability. Add to that a high level of energy and perseverance. If you don't have these things, it would require extraordinary training to get you into the big leagues. And where do you go for your integrity lesson?

Even if you are a natural in many of the factors, you have to keep working at it. My great ones never stop. If a person has extreme determination and the unbending will to succeed, they can learn some of the qualities. But to do so, they have to want to succeed.

And now again, the same type of question. Take strategy design and development for instance. If this is really important in our business, why aren't we teaching it? Why aren't we offering it at our seminars? We are at the business of strategy and strategic design all the time. It is what makes our work the great challenge and adventure it is. How do you approach a prospect? How do you build the strongest case? Which is the right button to push? How do you get their attention? What is the most effective way possible to get the gift and have the prospect feel that there is no greater joy possible than providing the gift? All of this is a part of the art of strategy.

Psychologists say that given a second chance, people will perform just about the same as they did the first time. And probably make the same mess of life. Behavior modification can happen but it requires determination. B.F. Skinner says: "We shouldn't try to change people. We should change the environment in which they live."

Since time began, many philosophers have told us that we can control our own destiny. We can become a different person. But they didn't tell us how to do it or how difficult it would be. "Of course I can give up smoking. I have given it up a thousand times."

No one can determine for you whether it will be worth the strain and struggle. The decision will be yours. None of this is a question easily answered. It is somewhat akin to what was said of Moses by an ancient court. The accusers said that Moses was cruel, greedy, self-seeking, and dishonest. One of the judges looked at Moses, puzzled, confused, and asked him if it could possibly be true what they had heard. "That was at one time. That's what I was once made of. I fought against it and that's how I became what I am."

You can do it. You can be your best possible self. You've got to finally do something about a concern or a problem to make it count. You must turn it into an opportunity. You will not be able to achieve greatness in each of the factors, but with the proper motivation and desire, you will be your greatest possible self.

As I wrote this book, I thought of some of the great leaders of the past. David Church, Sy Seymour, Arnaud Marts, Carlton Ketchum. It may be too soon yet to add John Schwartz and George Brakeley to the "Fundraiser's Hall of Fame," but their names surely belong. Some of these great people of fundraising, their names roll like thunder.

I asked myself: "Where are the really great fundraisers? Where have all the heroes gone?" I suspect they have gone with the less complex, the uncomplicated answers of a different era. It was probably easier than it is now. But these great ones, they led the way.

In actuality, there is no lack of heroes today. What we have is a realization that every man and woman can come into his or her own and has the full capacity of making a success out of life and career.

Some come by their talents naturally, and for them life is simpler. Still, they put in the hours and are willing to run the race. For those less endowed, it is clear that they can reach their full potential, but only with the passion and zeal that joins commitment together with action.

What will be required is discipline and will. No pain, no gain. You can truly be anything you want. You can reach your highest potential. You can achieve any level of success you chose. You will be able to say: "I have found my hero. And he is me."

****

14   The Verities

"There are three irrefutable rules which will assure your success as a fundraiser. Unfortunately, no one has ever discovered what they are."

                                                           —*John Russell*

"There are more secrets in my trade than in most . . . inseparable from its very nature. But there is much that we do not yet know."

                                                           —*Thoreau*

"Even if you reject this book, it will have served its purpose—which is to clarify your thinking and feelings. You will at least know what you don't like and are unwilling to accept—and that's a gift of sorts."

                                                    —*Rita Mae Brown*

Is there a "fundraising type"? Outgoing, people-oriented, backslapping, extremely well organized, goal oriented, brilliant. A combination Auntie Mame and Lee Iacocca. This magnificent creature probably doesn't exist. It's really hard, perhaps impossible, to know what makes an ideal fundraiser. If you were designing the perfect fly-catcher, you probably wouldn't design it to look like a frog!

I interviewed nearly 50 men and women I consider to be among the greatest in the country—each, the ultimate *fundmeister*. They are all winners. You are at once struck with the great diversity among them. They are tall and short, young and old, thin and not so thin, mellow and fierce, and from all parts of the country. They certainly do not seem to fit any simple cookie-cutter mold.

In fundraising, the competent and dynamic development officer has a unique combination of talents, attributes, and skills. The most effective ones are identified by both what they are and what they can do. But agencies and organizations, hospitals and colleges, symphonies and museums—they often have very particular requirements, specific needs and concerns, and special constituencies. I doubt one "perfect" fundraiser can fit every situation.

It's easy to define the qualities that are necessary—and probably incorrect!

When one of the supposed giants in our field complained to a friend about the shortage of really great fundraisers in the country, the friend replied: "There's probably one fewer than you think."

When I finally got the list down to where I wanted it, there were 30 factors and qualities that I tested. I discovered that the titans in our field often have a ravishing marinade of these skills and talents. When I discussed the list with W.A. Criswell, he said: "You can't be a soul-winner, a builder, and a money raiser without all of these attributes. They are all important. It is hard to choose among them, and I wouldn't know what to add."

What makes some succeed and others fail? This is the issue that gnaws. This is the overriding question.

What are the secrets, the mysteries? What profound bits of wisdom explain why one person racks up one fundraising success after another, while someone else lives out a humdrum career and existence? Why do some simply never make it? The best that some can boast of is what the fellow said after the Presbyterian minister's scathing sermon on the congregation's many sins. "Well, at least I haven't made any graven images."

The simple fact is there probably are no gimmicks or tricks. No road signs that can direct you down that path—no yellow brick road to Oz. And there may not be any special magic at all. Some factors, however, can provide the illumination, the light. We know it takes something greater, something surging inside ourselves.

Here's one quick and easy explanation that seems to sum it all up. Success takes common sense, the ability to communicate effectively and easily, the talent to motivate people, a good memory, and the hunger to succeed. The craving to succeed, the drive and determination to win may be most important of all.

What makes some exceptional? What sets them apart from others? What factors distinguish them—when men and women of seemingly equal talents continue to struggle along, some in ruts of mediocrity? You can't tell from outward appearances, no answer there. The really successful ones may be aggressive, good communicators, have presence, and be tranquilly self-confident. But on the other hand, they may be very quiet, not of sartorial splendor, and without sparkle or wit. I console myself with the thought that some runners are sprinters and some run the marathon—and both are valued in their own contest.

The list of characteristics that lead to winning could be virtually endless. Certain key factors, however, seem to be consistent with the great ones I have interviewed and known. These elements and characteristics shine as a beacon for others to follow.

I collected and examined the questionnaires returned to me—nearly 3000 in all. I spent a day interviewing the 50 great fundraisers—with a few, several days. I have been around this slippery, greased track for many years—and have worked directly, one-on-one, with probably close to 1000 men and women in this field.

What I offer here are some observations and findings about fundraising and fundraisers—the verities of our profession. Canons to work by. Tenets you can count on. These are truths and principles that will assure your being the best you can be.

I can defend each verity beyond challenge. If I have missed anything, I'm frankly surprised. I know how immodest the claim, but I have shared this list with a number of people and I have reviewed it with most of the great ones in my sampling —and they made no additions. The list is *sui generis*—unique of its kind.

It's a potpourri. I have listed these at random, with no order of priority. Most of the items are of equal importance. On a scale of 1 to 10—they're all tens. A few are elevens! They're off the graph.

Here they are, the verities. Sixty-three in all. Each important. Many, a virtual strike of lightning.

I remember once suggesting to one of our clients that he should consider attending a conference I thought sounded good. But he said: "What's the use? There's really nothing new there. I've heard all of this stuff before and I know most of it." And I said: "If you know so much, why aren't you doing something about it." We were never quite the same friends after that. And he still didn't attend the conference! And as far as I can tell, he's still doing his work in the same lackluster way.

To you, now, I can say: Do something about it! The verities are here, yours for the taking.

The point to keep in mind is that the list must not be discouraging to anyone. That would defeat the purpose of this book. No one will be able to claim each verity as his own. The question you need to answer for yourself is how you can make the very most of the talent and skills that you have. How can you best play the hand you have been dealt! How can you be the best you can possibly be!

The Verities

1. Common linkage appears to connect all of the great fundraisers. You have high ambition, are driven to achieve, and have immense inner-motivation. There is a very high level of optimism, a medium to medium-high intelligence level, a willingness to work long and hard, and what can only be termed "a robust ego." You are self-confident.

2. You read. You read everything in sight. You read incessantly and compulsively. In a recent study of 1500 of the nation's highest achievers, one of the factors they seem to have in common is that they read more books than the average—23 books a year. And you read magazines, newspapers, and professionals journals.

William McGowan is founder and chairman of the Board of Control Data. He is a voracious reader who plows through books, business publications, newspapers, general-interest periodicals, and specialized newsletters. An associate remembers when McGowan dropped in on him unexpectedly for a weekend visit in Florida. Soon after McGowan arrived, a box was delivered which was stuffed with magazines, reports, company memorandum, and books—that McGowan pursued as he floated in the swimming pool.

3. You are undaunted. There is no goal you can't achieve, no mountain you can't climb. Nothing is a road block or a problem. It's only a new opportunity, an exciting hurdle. It's faith and action. You decide, dare, do. Your life's philosophy, professionally and personally, is: "I Can Do It." There's no such thing as a casual attempt. Try? There is no try. There is only do or not do. And in truth, there is simply no "not do." There is brazen belief and fiery faith in the possible—anything can be done. You can do it, and even more divine—you understand that you must.

4. Above all, is triumph. The ultimate challenge is not to endure, but to prevail. You accept that challenge and win great victories for yourself and your institution.

5. Creative planning wins. You cannot increase the size or the quantity of the gift—without enhancing the incisiveness of the planning and the decisiveness of the strategy. Planning is the seed from which winning takes root and grows.

There are times that to gain, you must yield. In developing strategy, you look into the future through a rear view mirror. For instance, you read a book from the beginning to the end. But you develop a fundraising strategy the opposite way—you start with the end, the objective you wish to achieve, and then you do everything you must to reach it.

Admit it! At times you feel like the little boy with a big dog—waiting to see where the dog wants to go so he can take you there. Doing the research for a top prospect is like looking for a black cat in a dark room. Developing the strategy for making the call on the top prospect is like looking for a black cat in a dark room—in which there is no cat. Finally, making the call on a top prospect is like looking for a black cat in a dark room in which there is no cat and someone yells: "I got it!"

6. You are a communicator. Peter F. Drucker was quoted in a recent edition of *The Wall Street Journal.* What he said about leadership is immediately transferrable to our profession of fundraising. Drucker says that the responsibility of an effective fundraiser is thinking through his organization's mission, defining and establishing it, clearly and visibly. You must be able to communicate clearly and compellingly the goals of your organization and its priorities. You set and maintain the standards. Your first task is to be the trumpet that sounds a clear and dramatic sound. It must be a resonant call to action.

7. Success is always coupled with perseverance. An unrelenting persistence. It is a key element. George Sand was no fundraiser but in one of her famous letters, she wrote quite a remarkable definition of success appropriate to our field: ". . . Simple taste, a certain degree of courage, self-denial to a point, and love of work. And determination and patience. Persistence and perseverance." Success is elusive, never fully achieved or final. Nor is failure totally flawed or total. But the highest level of success depends on the courage to pursue the chase with diligence.

Several years ago, winners of the Horatio Alger awards for outstanding accomplishments in business were asked to name the factors which contributed to their success. Their response was "faith, hard work, belief in people, and service to others." But in a deeper investigation, the single most important answer was—motivation, inner-drive, and persistence. It is the final payoff. Those Horatio Alger winners, they could all have been fundraisers!

We in fundraising understand that success is a long race, conducted in inches. We face rejection and refusal head-on and respond with even greater dedication and determination.

8. This one is obvious: You ask for the order. Markita Andrew is 13 years old and she gives us the answer. She is the champion seller of Girl Scout cookies—12,000 boxes last year. She has led the country the last several years. She says: "You can't just stand around and chat. You've got to lean forward, look them in the eye, and ask for the order." That's it—you've got to ask for the order.

Ronald Steel wrote a biography of Walter Lippman. He asked Lippman why he gave all of his papers and memorabilia to Yale. He was afterall a graduate of Harvard, a member of the Harvard Board of Overseers, and he always assumed that Harvard would want his papers. According to Steel, Harvard, in its usual way, assumed it would get his papers. But it never formally approached him. It never asked him. And here's the moral for all of us: Yale asked for them and it got them. It even got his beloved baseball hat!

9. You are high-touch, low tech. You have a great appreciation for all of the latest electronic equipment available, but you understand that the computer does not take the place of calling on someone personally for a gift—not anymore than a pencil substitutes for literacy. But you understand, also, that writing without a pencil has its own complications! Milton Murray sums it up best of all. "One of the most significant changes in our field is the new development in high technology. High-tech, low-touch is what many of our people are about these days. We have to work against that. We need the personal touch. If we lose that, it becomes just a business, not a ministry."

The techniques of the business are not important. The technicians know "how." But that's not the heart and soul of our work. You must know the "why."

10. Great fundraisers are winners. They have a lust and a will for winning. Their attitude seems to be that if you want to be in second place, nobody is going to fight you for it! We attempt nothing great unless there are difficulties to overcome. We persevere and achieve from our desire to win and from the pride we have in vanquishing all.

11. You have decisive resolve. Nothing significant has ever been accomplished unless some man or woman dreamed it should be done. Someone believed it could be done. And then, most importantly, someone decided that it must be done.

12. You delight in the premise that fundraising provides fulfillment to deeds not words. It forces us to believe in the promise of the future, but it pays great tribute for what we achieve today. It chastens mistakes, but it is forgiving. It pays great dividends to those who strive the most, run the race, and give the best they have in them. And every day is a new adventure. That is the promise.

13. You have presence. None of the men and women I interviewed indicated that presence was important—and then most of them spend a good bit of time talking about how important an element this actually is!

For the type of fundraising I've been writing about, being "attractive" to the donor is important. Having "the right" physical appearance is part and parcel of the whole collage which confronts the donor. This certainly doesn't mean being pretty or handsome. That has nothing to do with it. And it doesn't mean having "a power handshake," or being a roaring extrovert.

Almost every one I interviewed said something very akin to what George Engdahl told me: "I think that the way we dress and the way we look is important. I wouldn't want anyone calling on me who wasn't well groomed and well put together.

They need to look alive and vital. And I think they need to be terribly careful about their weight. A great deal of this is something that each person has considerable control over."

Having presence was rated at the bottom of the list of factors—next to the very last. No one thought it was important, and everyone talked at length about it!

We all know a man or woman—who on entering a room, makes the room a little less crowded! I don't believe that this type can make it in our field, at least not at the high level of success we've been discussing. Not unless there is sufficient inner-motivation to do something about it. To have presence that fills the room. It attracts others to you. It helps get the gift.

Presence is one of those words that everyone talks about, and no one defines. It somehow eludes precise description. Yet, it's one of the most important elements in our work. I've tried to put my finger on what it is—this ethereal quality. If there is one single factor that explains it best of all, it would be charisma. Yes, I know! I'm sorry to use that overworked word, but that depicts it best of all. Charisma, before the Kennedy era, was a beautiful term, from two Greek words—a divine gift of grace. The energy, the force, the vigor. It's not physical appearance, dress, or funny stories. The single quality that sets those "who have it" apart from those who don't—is energy. That's presence: Energy. Divine, invincible energy. It shows and its glows.

14. Boldness has genius, power, and magic to it. The courage to dare, to step out—that's what wins the contest and gets the gift. The great fundraisers are infused with boldness and courage. An awesome audacity. There must be the willingness to brave the unexplored—and to attempt the unthinkable. The challenge! The great ones in this business thrive on it. It is the one button to push to get them started, and running.

There is a glowing, glorious statement about courage in Theodore Roosevelt's *The Men In The Arena*. He says that the credit belongs to the man who is actually in the arena, who strives valiantly, who errs and comes up short again and again—because there is not effort without error. At best, he knows in the end the triumphs of high achievement and at the worst, if he fails, at least fails while daring greatly. His place shall never be with those whose cold and timid souls know neither victory nor defeat.

15. You have an unwavering commitment to the institution, and a near-militant belief in its mission. Goethe wrote: "Until one is committed, there is hesitancy, the chance to drop back, always ineffective. The moment one definitely commits oneself, then Providence moves, too. All sorts of things occur to help one that would never otherwise have occurred."

Your commitment to the institution must be unshakable. That doesn't mean without question or constructive challenge. That would be faith without thought. But your commitment to the cause must glow and glitter for all to see.

The Salvation Army was founded by an extraordinary person, a zealot, who asked: "Why should the devil have all of the good songs?" It was Booth's unmitigated commitment to the cause and his unbounded belief in the army's mission that made the growth of this organization possible.

16. You have a quality of leadership. Something quite distinctive is in evidence in those who are successful in the field—a special quality of leadership. You sense it, you somehow see it, you can almost feel it. It is kindred to the characteristic of "presence," but it's really more than that. It didn't rate high on the list, yet everyone spoke about it.

Father Hesburgh came as close as anyone. "I'll tell you what I feel leadership is all about. As far as I'm concerned, I bring a vision of where I want to go and I am able to communicate it. That's what it's all about. Having a great vision and being able to communicate it. That's what it's all about. Whatever it is that I seem to do, and I'm not certain what that is, it does seem to say: 'follow me.' You've got to lead the way and take the action. If you want to attract volunteers and dollars, you have to exhibit a quality of leadership—and people will be attracted to you. I am convinced that donors like to put their money on people and institutions that they really believe in. I somehow communicate a sense of leadership, and people are willing to follow me. I do not say this in any boastful way. It just seems to be what happens."

17. If you can conceive it, you can achieve it. The surest way to guarantee success: determine you will succeed. You envision it. You dream of it. You will it to happen. That's how you win. That's the road to success. You're the kind of person who goes after Moby Dick with a rowboat, a harpoon, and a jar of tartar sauce!

18. You understand that every grand opportunity is simply masquerading as a problem, a mystery waiting to be solved. If you don't understand the problem, then explain it to someone and listen to yourself discussing it. Make certain that you never state a problem in the same terms as it was originally brought to you. Studying the reverse always helps. Don't worry about an approach that transforms one problem into another—you're probably taking the first step towards an exciting solution. If the answer seems to be surprising or even off the wall, it's probably useful! And if you seem to hit the bull's-eye each time with one of your solutions, you're either coming up with the wrong answer once in a while, or the target's too near.

19. You inspire others to action. A fundraising program or project must be pursued with inspiration by the fundraiser. It is important to note that as significant as it is, inspiration alone provides only passion and spirit to a program. But without unyielding action, it is lifeless. If inspiration is the rudder, action is the engine that propels the program. Inspiration must be combined with action in defatigable proportions. I call this phenomenon: Inspiraction. Add the word to your vocabulary! To be successful, you must have unlimited inspiraction.

20. You must stand on tiptoes! You reach for the stars. Your sights must be lofty and soaring. High expectations impel and drive action. Behind the enthusiasm, the inspiration, the passion, there must be the willingness to accept high expectations. The joy and the exhilaration of the challenge. You can choose. You can decide. You can will it to happen in your special way. When you set towering expectations, nothing can prevail against you. You will win. It is up to you to plant the seeds for audacious expectations. Don't reach for what you can. You must reach for what you cannot!

21. You can be satisfied—but only with the very best. You are built for fight or flight. On a regular basis, you review your objectives and achievements. You need praise and recognition to further motivate them. There is an inner-reward that keeps them going—but recognition is important. And it comes from either outside sources or within. But it comes.

There is another group. For them, there is no change. Content and complacent, they are satiated with their state and status. No matter how great the motivation, they are satisfied with their lives. They may be immensely happy with their personal life, having great fun with their leisure, and enjoying life to the fullest. And that is good. But if they are satisfied and content with their professional production, they will not be great fundraisers. The successful ones live in a constant state of dissatisfaction. You want to win. You feel it down deep. You understand that to be a good loser is to be a loser. You are driven by your goals and objectives. The motivation comes from within. You combine momentum, passion, and a need for market position. You are intensely competitive.

22. You know it has to benefit the donor. It's easier to sell a program or a project if you are benefit-oriented. That should be your entire focus. Buck Rogers, the marketing guru of IBM, said: "At IBM, we don't sell products—we sell solutions." Few people buy a project, no matter how altruistic they might be. Not if there isn't some benefit to them. Even the highest level of altruism is selfish to a great extent—it does provide benefit to the donor. You've got to give your prospects WIIFM—What's In It For Me! You can secure most any gift you seek, if you help a prospect get what they want.

23. Perfection is not a perfect solution. There is a significant difference between striving for excellence and attempting perfection. With the proper attitude and determination, the first is attainable, gratifying, and healthy. The latter is virtually impossible and frustrating. Perhaps even neurotic. It also happens to be an extraordinary waste of time. The difference between excellence and perfection goes virtually unnoticed and almost certainly will not cause either you or the institution to lose or win a gift. But the cost of pursuing perfection is enormous. Those who make a fetish out of perfection ravage precious resources that should be allocated more effectively somewhere else. Those of you who are best in this field follow a system of "sensible approximation." You don't settle for anything short of the best you can do. But you don't waste time, either, worrying if it is not sheer perfection. Striving for perfection is an impossible and debilitating state of mind in an imperfect world.

24. You must sacrifice. Our work is demanding and may require severe compromises in your life. Reaching your objective is knowing what it is others want—the WIIFM (What's In It For Me) Theory. But to be successful also requires knowing what you want. And what you are willing to give up to get it. There is always the sacrifice. The best work is most often done under duress and at great personal cost.

25. You work hard, think big, listen carefully. Ben Feldman says only three things count. Listen to Ben Feldman, he should know! There are more than 1600 life insurance companies in America and Ben Feldman, by himself, has written more insurance than 1000 of the companies. He has been the leading salesman for New York Life for more than two decades, and has set all of those records in East Liverpool, a little town on the Ohio River. What he says is at the very core for all of those of us in fundraising. His three secrets for success are: Work hard, think big, and listen very well.

26. The quality of the experience is what counts. Experience is important—but it is most certainly not the number of years that count, it is the quality of experience. And most important, it is that magnificent combination of characteristics and skills that you bring to your experience that makes good fundraisers into great ones.

27. You practice the principle of ready, fire, aim. Some in our field are guilty of spending all of their time preparing for a campaign, or analyzing the most effective way to call on a prospect, or evaluating their plans. They never seem to have time to actually go out and make the call for a gift. They are joyously busy spending their time analyzing and assessing. I call this grave disease: "Analysis paralysis." The prognosis is not good. The patient will almost certainly pass away, or eke out their profession in the most lackluster sort of way.

28. Your life is encircled with objectives. You are goal-driven, and goal-oriented. You are blessed! Lee Iacocca says that nothing is better than a life and death struggle to get your priorities stright. Without daring and ambitious aspirations, you will be uninspired, and without destination or destiny. Objectives are dreams—visions with deadlines.

29. Details guide and gird your work. "God is in the details," said Meis Van der Rohe. And to be successful, you understand how essential details are to achieving the highest level of excellence. And that means getting the gift! But you also understand that details don't mean the minutia and the mechanics of our work. Details, to you, mean having everything precisely in place that will provide the optimal opportunity of getting the gift.

30. You have focus. There is the excruciating sharpness and preciseness of perfect focus. A single-mindedness on an objective. Nothing gets in the way. There is a stabbing stubbornness about letting go.

31. No pain, no gain. There is a willingness, even an eagerness and expectation, to pay the price—whatever the cost. There has to be sacrifice to be successful in this field. No pain, no gain. It requires intense motivation. Long hours, long days. For days, with what seems no end. There is the mental stress, the emotional anguish, the physical strain—it is a never-ending contest. But somehow, there seems to be only joy and exhilaration. The great ones are nuts! You seem to be willing to pay the price, and you love it!

32. You recruit the strongest. Build around you the greatest, the most effective people. Not only staff, but volunteers. Particularly with volunteers, recruit those who are leaders in their field, who are themselves driven by the passions and qualities that make one successful. You'll be amazed at how much you can accomplish by learning, listening, and following. And if you don't care who gets the credit, you will be able to accomplish unbelievable achievements. The strongest in our field recruit the strongest to work with. You can always tell the caliber and character of a development officer by the people he or she recruits. If the volunteers are weak, you can be almost certain you have a weak development person. The "amateur" in fundraising is more necessary than ever. By amateur I refer to the Latin meaning of the word: lover. Find, seek, recruit the strongest volunteers and you will find, like any good lover, they give back in return much more than they receive.

And don't be misled by what you've heard about board chairmen and volunteers. Behind the cold, austere, severe exterior—there beats a heart of stone!

33. Follow my rules of the eight "I's." If you have five of this group, you'll be good in this field. If you have seven or

eight, you're almost certain to be great! Here are the eight "I's":
Integrity, Instinct, Intelligence, Imagination, Intestines, Irrever-
ence, Intensity, and "Inthusiasm"!

34. Wait to worry. It's probably the best advice you can
follow in life—from both a personal and professional standpoint. To begin with, most of the things we worry about simply
never happen. Worrying is the single most unrewarding of all
human emotions. It tears you down, it tears you apart. And
worst of all, it doesn't accomplish anything. If you've come
across a problem with a prospect, you have to deal with it.
Worrying won't solve the problem. If it doesn't look like you're
going to be able to meet budget, worrying won't help. If you're
not going to make the campaign goal, worrying won't help you
reach it. What is required is some creative problem solving.

35. Your dictum is grow or go. Peak performers live
with high uncertainty and constant change and seem to take it in
stride. You continue to learn. For you, it's a continuing process
of "grow or go." You live in a constant state of self-renewal. You
have the capacity to acknowledge errors, and treat them as
learning experiences. You are curious and you learn from everything, even failures—even though this can be a source of personal embarrassment. You are enthusiastic, and it is contagious.
They do everything with energy and commitment. For you, the
pulse beats high—and it is always the spring of life, no matter
what your age. You continue learning, reaching, seeking, probing. And growing.

36. You never have enough time. Never! High
achievers would like to spend a lot of time just sitting with
their feet propped on a desk, and thinking. But you don't—
there simply isn't the time. You all crave more time for thinking
and just plain dreaming—but your lives and schedules are too
filled for that. You all carry the heavy burden of feeling there is
so much to do and so few hours in the day to do it. Your ocean is
so big; your rowboat is so small. You abhor procrastination and

consider it the art of keeping up with yesterday. You are jealous
with your time and you guard it with your life. And what you
want most of all, the greatest present possible, is to have 27
hours to the day, and eight days to the week. You understand
how to use your time most efficiently and gift-effectively, like
packing a suitcase—small things in small places. And your bag is
packed to the fullest. Time is life.

37. You seek role models. Look for men and women to
pattern your life and work after. In one of Martin Burber's
books, he speaks of the saying of the wise rabbi of the first
century: "The good Lord has so created Man that everyone can
make every conceivable mistake on his own! Don't ever try to
learn from other people's mistakes. Learn what other people
do right."

There's the story of the second grader who wrote an essay
on the life of Socrates: "Socrates was a philosopher. He went
around pointing out errors in people and the way things were
done. They fed him hemlock." Learn from what others do
right—and you will be establishing your course on the map of
success. Adopt an error-embracing mode—make errors your
friends, embrace them and learn from them. Follow this dictum
and I promise you that even your errors will be remembered
someday with pleasure.

38. Common sense is a prime requisite. One of the
major differences between the non-achiever and the peak performers is that the latter master the art of applying the obvious.
Common sense is essential. As far as common sense is concerned, nothing succeeds like excess. You can't have too much. It
is perhaps one of the leading factors in winning the gift. It enables
you to analyze a very complex situation and somehow develop a
solution and design which cuts through the fat and gets to the
very nub of the situation. It turns out that common sense is not
so common at all. It's the ability to discern the facts from the
fancy. High intelligence is not critical, common sense is.

39. You know the twelve characteristics most important to success. These are identified by George Gallup, Jr. in a study he conducted among 1000 men and women he considered to be "the most successful in their field." They are listed in the order of their priority.

- Common sense
- Special knowledge of your field
- Self-reliance
- General intelligence
- Ability to get things done
- Quality of leadership
- Knowing right from wrong
- Creativity and inventiveness
- Self-confidence
- Oral expression
- Concern for others
- Luck

40. Creativity and innovation depend heartily on trust. It means that you trust your instincts, and you have the courage to pursue vigorously your intuition. There is both a common sense and a sixth sense. The latter has a great deal to do with creativity. Marvin Minsky said that you don't understand something until you understand it more than one way. Creativity is the ability to join one idea to another, and come up with a new answer. It's old ideas into new combinations that win. Put your imagination into over-drive. It is doubtful that anyone has had a totally original idea. The repotted flower grows the highest and healthiest.

41. You have a concern for people—a compassion, a love. The pull is so strong, it is nothing less than ministerial in its approach and commitment.

42. You have a great joy in what you are doing, a love affair. In one of his speeches, Will Rogers said: "If you want to be successful, it's pretty simple. There are only three things to keep in mind. It's really that easy. Know what you are doing. Love what you are doing. And believe in what you are doing." Some think of fundraising as "the profession of pain." Those few will not make it. In one of her great novels, Rebecca West wrote: "Life ought to be a struggle of desire towards adventures whose nobility will fertilize the soul. To avoid the passion is the impulsive death. Sterility is the deadly sin. To be successful in your work, you must abandon yourself to your passion." We in this business are one with Thoreau, joined together, and "carved out of the breath of life itself."

I am certain that success is due less to experience than ardor. Less to intelligence than zeal. Less to the mechanics of the job than enthusiasm. The winner is always the one who gives body and soul, totally and unreservedly, to the joys and passion of the task.

43. You are unremittingly opposed to status quo. There are no valid rules, only new ventures and opportunities to explore. Those who like rigid order, defined resources, and abundant staff—they will not make it. Those who rely on structured systems, processes and procedures—they'll have a hard time.

44. You love calling on people. You enjoy most aspects of your work—but calling on people, confronting them with the immense opportunity to share in great works and deeds—for you, that's the pinnacle.

45. You understand that survival is inherent to our profession. Never let yourself get between a dog and a lamp post! That should be our credo! The reward of energy, enterprise, and success—is surviving for another year. At times, even a pink slip! Our tombstone should read: I was expecting this, but not so soon.

You understand about survival. At times the secret of keeping your job is to keep the five guys who want to fire you away from the five guys who haven't made up their mind yet. But something constructive is always born out of adversity.

It doesn't seem fair at all, but no one said life was fair. "Nothing so focuses the mind," says Dr. Samuel Johnson, "as the knowledge that one is to be hanged the following morning." You achieve your high objectives one year, but you are measured by next year. The board remembers the past, but they relish the present, and cherish the future. Victor Hugo tells the story of the sailor who was commended and given a medal for extraordinary heroism in capturing a cannon rolling around loose on the deck of his warship. Then he was hanged for his negligence in allowing the cannon to become loose from its moorings in the first place.

You may not be pleased with this day-to-day surveillance, but you accept the process as part of your work. It is imposed and impressed on you. You perform a high trapeze act every day—and without a safety net. Every once in a while, you pull off a triple somersault. That makes the dare worth the doing.

46. You pull up the roots to see if the flower is still growing. Many of us grew up repeating the ditty: Patience is a virtue, virtue is a grace—grace is a little girl who wouldn't wash her face! But in fundraising, impatience is a virtue. You are never satisfied. You have a very low tolerance with the pace of your program and the progress. You are itchy by nature! You do not suffer easily standing still or treading water. It's the race you favor, and most of all, the winning.

47. You are men and women of ideas and ideals. Your beliefs are lofty. You continue to reach higher and higher, and you are spurred on to better and more significant things. You understand that your ideals represent true force and energy. It is the foundation which prods you to greater achievement. Arnold Toynbee said that apathy can only be overcome by enthusiasm, "and enthusiasm can only be aroused by two things: first, an ideal which takes the imagination by storm; and second, a definite intelligible plan for carrying that ideal into practice."

48. You are results-oriented. Your entire focus is on the solution and the outcome. You come from the Try-harder School, and you understand that you are graded on many factors, but the greatest of these are results. And that constitutes your final report card.

49. It takes rigorous discipline. You have a huge reservoir of will and determination. Discipline in all you do—your time, your priorities, your attention to myriad details that make a successful program. Discipline propels dreams and visions and action into success.

50. You have soaring spiritual values. Somewhere in your background, in your early childhood, there was a value system—both stringent and joyful—that was imposed upon you. Church and prayer were very likely a part of your early days.

51. Memory is monumental. Most of the great fund-raisers I interviewed have extremely well organized offices, clean desks, and work by rigid schedules. Time is your god. But what stands out most is your remarkable memory. You never forget anything. Especially regarding prospects, donors, and everything to do with the raising of gifts. You bring together a glorious combination of energy, hard work, a sense of history, and exceptional powers of evocation—and a magnificent memory. That, and the inability to be boring!

52. You have a high degree of self-confidence. As they say, you must be as confident as a Methodist with four aces.

53. You believe in the promise of tomorrow. *Carpe Diem* is an ancient Latin phrase which means, "Seize the day." You rejoice in the present because you know that the day is aglow with all the tomorrows.

54. You are delighted with the specialists in your field. You understand how important these men and women are to an effective development office. Those who have immense expertise in phonathons, research, computer technology, and response mail—they make things happen. You wouldn't be without them. But the great generalists rule the world. You seek broad men and women, sharpened to the point, who have an understanding and appreciation of all of the specialties—but who are unencumbered by them. You know how to use each specialty to your great advantage. You know a little bit about many things, but claim no specialty as your own. You revel in your overall understanding and expertise. You are a four-star Generalist!

55. You have a way of getting "yes" for an answer— even before you ask the question. Your ability to motivate is your vision and passion, put into action. It is the spark which turns into a mighty flame. It is what transforms a prospect into a donor. Being an effective fundraiser is the act of persuading a donor to want to do something you are convinced should be done. You understand your donors. You are sensitive to what compulsions drive them, what instincts dominate their life and giving. You know how to pull their heart strings. One thing is certain, unchangingly so: The fundraiser with the keenest insight for motivation understands what compels a donor to action. The ability to motivate.

56. Long tenure in a position is essential. You don't jump from job to job. You stay at your institution. How long? As long as it takes. And how long is that? Sufficient time to conceive the bold dreams develop the plans, know your constituencies, and achieve your objectives. Some say that if you are in a job too long, you get into a rut. But these "rutters" were very likely falling into place early in their work. For you, the challenge, the excitement, the adventure continues no matter how long you are at an institution.

57. You make your own luck. There is a saying that the harder you work, the luckier you get. But evidence suggests that some are luckier than others. Good fortune follows them. It isn't inadvertent. You plan for it and you seek it. You live by serendipity. You have the faculty of being at precisely the right place at exactly the right time. What assures luck is eternal vigilance to new opportunities, a restless spirit, and an irreverent attitude for the obvious.

58. Your work and life excite you—and it shows. Because you are happy in your life's work, you are more likely to be happy in your personal life.

59. You are charged with energy. There is a vigor and a vitality that is undeniable and indefatigable. You seem to be able to endure an assiduous workload, hour after joyous hour, and require very little sleep.

Forget everything you learned in high school physics about the description of "energy." In fundraising, the definition is: Success. It is a rare quality conferred on few. But all of the great ones seem to have it in abundance—an unlimited reservoir which seems never to ebb. Some men and women have it, some don't. A physician told me that it has something to do with the genes. But the great ones all exhibited this boundless energy. All were like tightly wound wire, ready to spring. Kinetic energy— it is man's main circuit board, from which flows the electricity that gives illumination and vision to the prospect.

It may perhaps be the major ingredient in the extraordinary mix that provides presence. Energy begets enthusiasm and is a first-cousin to charisma—that divinely inspired spark of leadership.

Each day, you all play at centre court at Wimbledon. You play, whether you're up to it or not. And you play to win. People seek those with energy. They respond to them. It is the pump from which flows the miracles and magic. It provides the power for all great action. Energy is infectious, creates invincible potency, and invigorates and inspires all around you.

60. The work burns like fire in your bones. Because your work is your mission, you become a zealous achiever.

Most of you are self-avowed workaholics. And you love it! You wear this as a badge of honor. To you, it isn't work, it is sheer joy.

Kemmons Wilson is the founder of Holiday Inns. He somehow never took time to get his high school diploma, but one year he was asked to return to the school he had attended to give the commencement address. He started off by telling the group that he was probably the wrong person to be talking to them because he never got a degree. He went on to say he really didn't have sage counsel to give them. "The only thing that really sets me apart from most men is that I've only worked half days my entire life—and that's really the best advice I can give you. You follow that—work half days every day. It doesn't matter which half—the first twelve hours or the second twelve hours."

61. Research is important, but action will prevail. Knowing precisely the proper strategic approach to a large potential donor is not at all a tidy process. You understand that. It takes an intuitive sense and feeling, it takes common sense, and it takes all the research possible. But it's important to remember that not everything that is true is provable. You must move forward, even if you do not have all of the research about a donor that you feel would be desirable. At times you can be strangled by facts and research. It is a prime example of Herbert Spencer's famous warning about "The murder of the beautiful theory by a brutal gang of facts." You depend on research, but you are not dependent on it. You shall move, persevere, and succeed. You know that research alone will not get the gift.

I know of one institution that has a glorious research component. It has been gathering detail and data about prospects for years. But it hasn't yet made its major calls. It's been getting ready for war, but hasn't yet waged it.

62. Listen—and you'll get the gift. All of the communication skills are valued. Most of all, you treasure verbal competency—for that is what helps motivate prospective donors to action. But these are the sending elements of communication. The most important of the communication faculties is that of listening. It is truly listening that inspires the gift.

Meaningful, creative silence! Listening is not passive, it is active. You know that if you give others what they want, you will get what you want. No other skill is as important. Vartan Gregorian says: "I think that the ability to communicate is essential. I am fortunate in that I feel I am a good speaker, a very good speaker. I can be persuasive. I can inspire. But most of all, the reason I feel I am successful, is that I am an unbelievably good listener."

For some in this field, there appears no evidence, empirical or otherwise, that the tongue is connected to the brain. It's hard for us to be quiet. Because of all the other traits that go into this business, it's not our nature. You have heard about people who talk too much—but you have not heard of anyone who listens too much. In fundraising, it is impossible to listen too much. It is what wins the gift.

63. Nothing is more important than integrity. Integrity is the *sine qua non* in our business. It is everything. It involves a moral imperative deep inside us. It's always there. It is not negotiable. It's a well-spring, and from it comes energy and commitment. It drives us on.

I can assure you that integrity is the mightiest weapon in your arsenal. Its power is explosive. It brings together uncompromising individualism and blinding honesty. And it must be combined, too, with compassion—for without grace and love, integrity is without heart and life.

Impeccable integrity is redundant. Something is either right or it is wrong. Integrity isn't impeccable. Integrity stands alone—requiring neither modifier nor moderation. In our business, integrity isn't everything. It is the only thing. Integrity alone is no assurance of the ticket to the top, but without it you can't even begin the journey. Without it, you are a cannon without ammunition. You are nothing.

15   The End of the Beginning

"If there's one statement true of every single living person, it must be this: He hasn't achieved his full potential."
       —Harry Truman

"There's no heavier burden than having great potential!"
       —Linus to Charlie Brown

"An author is allowed to say: This and that are so, and you should believe me. And an author is expected to say: My truth is the only truth that matters—not absolute truth, but my truth. And if you don't like it, you can lump it."
       —W. Somerset Maugham

About the time I was doing my final editing of this book, I got a call from one of the great fundraisers I had interviewed. George Engdahl. There was a sharp edge to his voice. He told me he had been fired.

"I just got fired."

Cripes! He had been fired. One of my great ones had been fired!

No, he hadn't quit. And he wasn't allowed the dignity of resignation. He was fired.

I was stunned. So was he. It wasn't much of a telephone conversation. I promised I would call him in a couple of days, as soon as we both got our heads screwed back on.

I'll tell you the truth. When George told me the news, I felt absolutely sunk. Shocked. My heart and grief went out to him. I could feel his pain and embarrassment in every bone of my body. But all of that lasted only about 30 seconds. And mind you, we're close friends.

My next thought—well, you probably guessed it. My next thought was: I've got to take every reference to George out of the book. This is going to be a terrible embarrassment to me.

It didn't take me long to forget about George! I was worried about me. And concerned about the book. And frankly confounded about those important theories I had expounded. I had been tried, and found guilty of what the Germans call: *Aufgeputz*—"Too much much."

I got to talking to Jack E. Williams about my dilemma. Jack is the tremendously effective vice chancellor at the University of Tennessee, a close friend, and a fellow endowed with a tremendous amount of common sense. Being from the south, sometimes with Jack there's more hominy than homily—but he's always a comfort and a help to talk with.

He told me about a fellow we both know. Jack said: "Karl and I were talking the other day, and he tells me that he's not a fundraiser, and never has been. 'I'm a manager,' says he. No wonder he hadn't done what he had hoped. We were looking for a fundraiser, and what we got was a manager."

That's the answer—that is what happened to George. And when I talked with him later, and spoke with several members of his board, it was confirmed. George is a fundraiser, one of the greatest I have ever worked with. It turns out in this case that what the institution wanted was a manager.

As soon as I began finding a clearing in all of the confusion, I realized what had happened. It was obvious. And I found out the board of the institution had been sending out warning-signals for the past several months. It wanted George to spend less time on fundraising, and more on managing his staff. It may or may not have been the right priority for that situation. That's not the point. What does count is that the board knew what they wanted. George's antennae had failed him—he hadn't picked up the signal.

I went back to my notes. I had pages and pages from my day with him. Shazam! It was all there. It was obvious. In many of his comments, it was clear that he felt keenly the frustration of not having sufficient time to work with his staff. It came out time and time again. It was also quite obvious, however, that his great love was making the call, the one-on-one contest, getting the gift. For him, that was life's joy. Every day, it was like coming to bat in the World Series. But the board wanted a manager. George wanted to be a fundraiser. The board won.

I made a decision. George stays in the book—he's one of the best I've known. He'd be at the top of just about anyone's list.

When I started this book, I had all of the answers. By the time I had completed it, I wasn't even sure of the questions.

This business with George taught me a valuable lesson. The great ones in our business fall into three major categories: Managers, teachers, and fundraisers. I have chosen the fundraiser for my exposition. I grant you many cross lines. A select few even exhibit prodigious qualities in all three categories. The thrust and focus of this book, however, is on the fundraiser.

Along the way of writing this book, I didn't win many friends! There's someone, for instance, I'm quite close to—a former client, and a friend of long standing. I consider him one of the most effective managers in the business. He is an inspiration to his staff. He recruits painstakingly, molds and guides his people, encourages them when appropriate—well, he does just everything right. He doesn't miss a trick. He happens to have extremely high visibility in our field, and all acknowledge that he's just about the best manager in the business. But at least in my experience, I have not seen him do much fundraising. And that's why he's not included among those I interviewed. It was my loss. He is one of the most verbal in the business, has been at it a long time, and has a tremendous handle on the philosophy of giving and what this stuff is all about. But I haven't seen him do much fundraising.

But as far as George is concerned, he stays in the book. He's a great fundraiser. And he's a survivor, too. There he was, on the high trapeze, way above the crowd. It was a tense and hushed moment. All eyes were on him. If anyone had told George the board didn't want a triple somersault, he hadn't heard it. He was high in the air, it was breathtaking. He completed the triple with that special twist of his but missed the bar coming down. Fortunately, this time there was a safety net. Knowing George, he'll climb right up again and keep practicing. Next time he'll be smarter. And he'll continue performing those grand feats of wonderment. Few are like him. He's a survivor, but this time he'll probably play it safer. Falling isn't much fun. And it's embarrassing.

George Abbott is the author of *Babies,* a controversial book. Not too long ago, he sent 500 copies of the book to a charity for one of their auctions. The auction committee accepted the books with a proper acknowledgement and appreciation.

Well, you know how things can go wrong and not always go according to plan. As it turned out, a member of the committee decided to read the book—and felt that it was not at all an appropriate one for their institution. The board of the organization met and decided to return the 500 books to Abbott.

He was furious. He was really upset. Abbott put all 500 books in his van, returned to the site of the auction, and burned the books in front of those in attendance. That's what he did—he poured gasoline all over the books and set them on fire.

The blaze spread, and soon four houses were on fire. It looked like they might be totally destroyed, but the fire department finally arrived. Abbott jumped in his van and gunned the motor. Before he got away, someone heard him say: "It's tough to be a writer nowadays." Hey, I can identify with that!

I really didn't start out to write a book. But now that I have, I must say it's been one of the greatest pilgrimages I have ever made. You've heard how the longest journey starts with the first bold step. Let me tell you how it all started.

I was involved in a search for a major institution and wanted to develop a list of skills and talents they might use in selecting precisely the right man or woman for their position. That's how it all began.

I went to my library, but there wasn't a book on the shelf that had any resource material or information on which skills and talents were important in our business. Nothing that would help me determine what makes a great fundraiser. And there was nothing in my file. In fact, there really isn't a book on the subject, not a chapter, barely a paragraph. I could find nothing.

So I decided to make up my own list of criteria. I got a bunch of index cards and started writing like crazy. A couple words on each card. By the time I finished, I had come up with 89 different factors that I felt were important. There was some redundancy, but not much. Some factors had only slight shades of differences—but I was pretty pleased with my list. I also recognized that I would have to do some heavy honing.

I took this long list, and I reviewed it with 15 professionals in our field. This group comprises the men and women I consider to be some of the very special and most astute in our business. About half included men who head professional consulting firms. The other half were men and women in the top position in major institutions in the country.

I had intensive discussions with each person, most lasting three or four hours. We reviewed each of the headings and made an evaluation and ranking of the factors. On the basis of this assessment, my original list was narrowed finally to the 29 factors used for the research and interviews for this book. The complete, long version of talents and skills, attributes and characteristics is listed in the appendix.

Without question, my list of characteristics and criteria can be challenged. I will agree that there could be longer or much shorter lists of virtues than the one I designed. I'm not seeking validation, but it is curious that in all of the polling I have done with both lists, I have not had more than a handful of suggestions to add. That's rather remarkable considering the nearly 3000 responses I had to the questionnaire. This does not necessarily mean that my final list is complete, but it would be fair to say that it is not far from it. Not one of the qualities, however, is by itself rare. Indeed, we all know people in the field who possess a number of them.

There was only one late addition, only one factor in the final format that was not on my original list. During one of the evaluation meetings, I was scolded for not having something which dealt with integrity. A serious oversight, I was told. I added it to the final list and went even one better—referring to it as "impeccable integrity." Impeccable, indeed. Now that's a great deal of integrity! As it turned out, that single factor is felt to be among the most important of all of those I listed.

Now mind you, up to this point, I still hadn't thought about writing a book. It did bother me that there wasn't anything on the topic that I could put my hands on, and I found it frustrating and of consternation that a subject as essential as this is to all of us in the field had somehow escaped a thorough treatment and careful analysis.

At this same time, I had a call from Sister Margaret. She heads a major medical center. "Jerry, I'd like you to come and visit us as soon as possible. We're having a great deal of trouble with Don. I don't think he knows what we're trying to accomplish here, and I don't honestly think he knows a lot about development work and fundraising. It's gotten to the point where Don and I aren't even talking. We've got to do something about it. I'd like you to come as soon as possible and see if you can help us, and maybe even help Don find a new job."

I knew Don well. He didn't have a lot of experience but I was certain that he could handle the job. What I couldn't understand was the strained relationship between Sister and Don. They had started out as great friends.

I made my visit, and almost as an afterthought, took with me my original list—the one that included 89 factors. During our discussion, she told me again that she and Don weren't communicating. "He just doesn't seem to know what the job is all about." Before leaving to talk with Don, I showed Sister my list of factors and asked her to check the five which she felt were the very most important for the development office of the medical center. She looked over the list, asked a few questions, and made her choices. I then went off to see Don.

Don was not in the best of moods. He knew that things weren't going well and that he was having problems with Sister. Perhaps terminal! He said to me: "I can't understand what's happening. I think I am doing a pretty good job and we seem to be raising a lot of money. But Sister Margaret and I aren't even talking anymore. I don't think she understands what this business is all about." We talked some more and then I showed him the list, and asked him to check the five factors he felt were the most important in his work.

I have changed the names of the two people in this story, but I assure you it is true. Both Sister and Don do indeed exist, and the scenario described is precisely what transpired. Let me tell you what happened when I looked at the criteria Sister had checked, and those of Don.

I put the two sheets together. I was astonished! There wasn't one single item they had checked in common. Not one. No wonder they weren't talking. They weren't communicating because neither one really understood what the other felt was important. Absolutely no common ground, not between those two.

That's when I decided on the book. That's the moment I felt the undeniable pull to develop my list into a book. Something brief and lively on this inescapable theme. I still couldn't fathom why there was nothing on the subject. Surely, there is nothing of greater significance to all of us in this profession than to determine the factors that are the soul and fiber of becoming a great fundraiser.

The journey began. The concept for the book took form and shape. I decided immediately that my entire focus would be on those on the firing line, men and women on the paid staff of organizations and institutions. I wasn't particularly concerned what their position might be, but I did want them somewhere on the paid staff. This ruled out volunteers—some of whom are extraordinary fundraisers. But then, that's the topic of another book! And I ruled out all men and women associated with professional consulting firms. It's those soldiers fighting the battles, that's where my focus was to be.

What makes a really great fundraiser? There was really nothing for me to look at. No books, no periodicals, no research, no documentation, no data. I was starting from scratch. And it was a glorious, joyous journey—from beginning to end.

For one thing, I used questionnaires. I took my short list, now down to 30 factors after adding "impeccable integrity," and sent it all over the country—to fundraisers of all sizes, shapes, and sorts, asking them to indicate the items they felt were most important. I asked them to check the ten most important criteria in making a great fundraiser. Nearly 3000 of the questionnaires were returned to me. I segmented those by the different types of organizations that these returns represented.

An important point—I asked each person to give me the names of two or three men or women who they felt were the most effective and the greatest in our field.

I made up my own list of men and women I felt were the strongest in our profession, the titans, the giants. In addition, I reviewed all of the names that had been suggested. And I chose a few from that group.

In all, I interviewed 48 men and women—each in depth, each over an extended time. In the case of most, I spent at least a day. I collected a tremendous amount of information, took notes until I was drowning in them, and asked each to check my questionnaire.

In the book, I have quoted only about a dozen of the men and women I interviewed. I could have used all, but I felt it would be more confusing than helpful. For those I did not use or quote in my book, it was most certainly not a case of their being less productive or saying less. That was hardly true. It was more a case of those I did use saying more. The ones I included, their comments were pithy, direct, and dramatic. They seemed to speak for everyone.

But note—the book is not about these great fundraisers, it is by them. They speak through me, and I through them. It's their hymn I sing, and I add the orchestration. My job is to be the mirror that reflects their utmost thoughts and uppermost feelings. I provide the likeness and the light for those who wish to follow—for those who wish to be the best they can be. Follow me.

****

There comes a time in the life of every book when you have to stop staring at blank sheets of paper, and start writing.

I've been taught that you shouldn't spend your time trying to teach a cat to sing. It just wastes your energy and annoys the cat. I decided early that this would be more than a "how-to book." I wanted it instead to deal with the who, what, when, and why. Not the mechanics, but the art of fundraising. I used the examples and quotations of those I refer to as "the great fundraisers" to tell the story, and they do that eloquently. But it is not their book. It is not a beauty and personality contest. It is a book about the art of fundraising.

My group is as good as they come. You could certainly add some, and they would be as good perhaps—but not better. My group speaks for the art and to the artists in our field. Sure, many of them were CEOs, as well as fundraisers. But without exception they see themselves essentially as fundraisers.

I would be dismayed by anyone who said that nothing is new here—"I already knew all of that." My reaction would be: If you already knew so much, why aren't you practicing it? I have a feeling that these fundraisers may never make it to the highest level of our calling. Some fundraisers have been known to wrest triumphant gifts from a prospect even when the prospects were unquestionably and firmly committed to giving to the cause in the first place!

Harry Truman said: "The only things worth learning are those you learn after you know it all." I am convinced that the true fundraiser is an extraordinary combination of manager, manipulator, inspirer, amateur psychiatrist, motivator, and arm-wrestler—with common sense added.

Institutions expect their fundraisers to be physically attractive, charming, courageous, creative, and with the wisdom of Solomon. They do not often come that way!

The most common characteristic of the peak performers is actually their diversity. They do not look alike or act alike. They are not as light bulbs—essential in times of need, but interchangeable! If anything, the one thing the great ones share in common is that they will not conform to any single stereotype.

What a selection committee finally gets in their fundraiser is not always what they see at the interview session—a resume and a perfect surface performance in an artificial situation. It may, and often does, select a person for precisely the wrong reason. The great ones do not necessarily make magnetic first impressions. But they do make repeated good impressions. They wear extremely well.

What I am about to give you are the characteristics and skills in their order—as indicated by the 48 I interviewed, the 3000 questionnaires that were returned . . . and yes, my own rating. These factors are like clothes: They should be made to fit only those men and women they are suited for. They are not for everyone.

The conversations and studies of the fundraisers I included in the book are not designed to produce results as if they were scientifically representative samples. In my judgment, my group is among the best. The very best. Perhaps some are just as good, but I doubt many would be better. This is not a book of quantitative findings. It was never meant to be. But here are the results, to be used as it best suits you. The list is yours for the taking, to be read, studied, and to be used to make you the best you can possibly be. The list—as Ross Perot wrote recently—is for "those people who are willing to step out in front, make decisions, accomplish great things, take risks, and accept responsibility for their life."

The Top Ten

The top ten characteristics, attributes, skills, and talents—as ranked by three categories.

2736 Men and Women In The Field	The Great Fundraisers	My Ranking
1. Be A Good Listener	Impeccable Integrity	Impeccable Integrity
2. Strong Communication Skills	A Good Listener	A Good Listener
3. Ability to Motivate	Ability to Motivate	Ability to Motivate
4. Be Creative	Love the Work	High Energy
5. A Self-Starter	Concern for People	Concern for People

6. Able to See the Big Picture	Hard Working	High Expectations
7. Have Perseverance	High Expectations	Love the Work
8. Ability to Inspire Action*	High Energy	Ability to Motivate
9. A People-Person*	Quality of Leadership	Have Perseverance
10. Well Organized	Have Perseverance	Presence*
11. Impeccable Integrity	Self-Confidence**	Quality of Leadership*
	Common Sense**	

* Tied
** Factors Not on List

David Ogilvy has his own list, one developed for his staff. The qualifications he looks for are these:

1. High standards of personal ethics.
2. Big people, without pettiness.
3. Guts under pressure, resilience in defeat.
4. Brilliant brains—not safe plodders.
5. A capacity for hard work and midnight oil—and enjoy it.
6. Charisma—charm and persuasiveness.
7. A streak of unorthodoxy—creative innovators.
8. The courage to make tough decisions.
9. Inspiring enthusiast—with thrust and gusto.
10. A sense of humor.

Ogilvy is considered the high priest of advertising. Note how closely his criteria approximate those for fundraisers. It was both somewhat surprising and fascinating for me to find that the factors are very much the same for leaders—no matter what the field. I really had hoped for some major differences. Distinctions would have marked this study well. But I didn't find major differences, no matter what the profession or discipline. Leaders are leaders!

Develop your own list—it's an important investment in designing your personal career and future. In the appendix, I've prepared a matrix you can use to list the factors you feel are important and at the same time evaluate yourself. I've also allowed for an assessment to be made by the person to whom you report, or for members of your board or committee. You be the judge: You can either fill out the form yourself or have others share in the evaluation. Or both. But do it. Make the appraisal and define for yourself a list of the priorities you feel are the most important in making you a winner, the best you can possibly be.

I am convinced that the appraisal should be used by an organization when seeking a new person for the development function. Have the selection committee and the chief executive fill out the form. Add them all together and you'll know precisely the person you're looking for. You'll have a near-mirror profile of the man or woman who is just right for you. Rate your candidates against the profile and you'll be able to rank them in exact order of preference for your situation. For the first time, you'll have a qualitative measure to guide you. I promise you, it works.

Checking the list of the top ten is tough. All 30 on the list are important. And there surely is a confluence and mixing of all of these factors that go into making a great fundraiser. They overlap, coincide, and connect. Together, they form a glorious and intricate intersection—all roads of which lead to winning. All of the factors form a paradigm which will demand of you the highest motivation and determination. If you are now successful, you almost certainly share many of these qualities. If you choose in favor of higher attainment, you will want to work on as many of these as you can.

How many of these qualities are inherent or imposed at an early age? How many of the factors can be learned? And of those. are we offering opportunities for learning them?

To get the answers, I spoke with two psychiatrists and a specialist in behavioral modification. I found that there are no easy answers. They disagreed on several important points. Wouldn't you know they couldn't agree? Let me tell you their general attitude—and then, you're on your own.

They told me that much of what makes us good in this business relates to our passion—for our work, our program, our concern for people, and the mission of our institution. The passion, the experts tell me is learned as a child. In a sense, you learned to let go of your inhibitions and controls.

They told me more. Creativity is learned as a child. You let your fantasies surface. Creativity can be stifled by emphasizing orderliness too much in a youngster. A child is curious, the curiosity is encouraged, and that leads to creativity. It's easy to strangle this quality. We suffocate the imagination of children in the schools and at home all the time. But everyone has the ability to be creative. You can learn it. You can learn to be creative in measurable proportions.

All of the communication skills can be learned. You can learn to be a good speaker and a good writer. For some, it will require an act of extraordinary determination, but it can be done. And as far as listening is concerned—listed as being of prime importance—it can certainly be learned. It is perhaps the most important and the easiest of the three communication skills to conquer.

Preseverance is something you learn early. A concern for people is "caught" young, usually at home.

The experts all believe in the importance of a role model, particularly one at an early age. Being a hard worker is learned somehow between the ages of 5 and 15, and usually by a role model in the home.

The more successful the personal life, the more successful the career. And the people at the top of their field usually have a spouse or a friend who is greatly encouraging and of immense support. People who aren't happy almost never do well in their work. And if you feel good about yourself and your job, you work hard.

You seem to be born with a high level of energy. You have it or you don't. You can enhance this quality with exercise and proper diet, but only in a minimal way. Very often, however, low energy is directly related to an unhappy personal life or to an unpleasant work situation and a struggle with the job. Being tired and low in energy, and sinking fast, are usually related to emotional stress. If there is joy and passion for your work, the long hours do not tire you.

Integrity is learned early. It can be changed, but only with an excruciating transformation, an act of determined will.

High expectations are set in place somewhere between ages 5 and 15. But these can be learned and encouraged.

Having presence is related to a number of factors, mostly inherent and learned, and acquired at an early age. Most people come pre-equipped in this regard. But the quality can be studied and enhanced.

I spoke to a sociobiologist. Yes, there is such a person! She told me that the ability to motivate is a social skill and is a message that can be learned.

All of the skills and factors can be moved a little one way or the other. It requires self-evaluation and self-renewal. The choice is yours. One of the psychiatrists told me that "success in life is only a point here or there." It only takes knowing what you want to be, and the determination to get there. There it is, yours for the taking, only a point, here or there.

I was surprised at the talents and skills listed as being most important. And not surprised at all! What really astounded me, though, was the number of characteristics innate and the qualities formed and shaped in our early years. I wasn't prepared for this. It was not what I expected, and frankly it's not what I wanted to find.

The great ones—their life's script was written for them at an early age. It doesn't seem entirely fair. They were born to raise. They would have been superior in almost any field, but in our profession—they were born to raise.

No one said life was fair, but this seems outrageous! What are the rest of us to do? We start by learning what our assets are, we embrace them, and we do everything humanly possible to enhance them. We examine the qualities where we have deficiencies. We make a commitment to change. We determine a plan, and we never let go. It's a life's struggle, and worth it.

I decided early on to pursue a career in fundraising. In this regard, I am unlike most in the profession. I knew from the moment I made my first call on a prospect that whatever was involved in this business, it was for me. I loved it! It embodied everything in life I cared about. I was born to raise.

That doesn't mean that I have the qualities necessary to make a great fundraiser. Far from it. But I can tell you this, I have never stopped working at them. I expect never to stop. Someday, I shall be on someone's list of "one of the great ones." I know I will. I am determined.

When I first went into the business, there were 320,000 not-for-profit organizations. Today, there are 740,000. That means that the competition for the philanthropic dollar is keener and more intense—more than ever. There are many more places for a donor to give, and more of us are calling on the donor—to help him, of course, make the right decision. And recruiting top volunteer leadership is more difficult. It's tougher than it has ever been. Your competition is getting smarter all the time. There are more of them, and they are better prepared. They're gaining on you and nibbling at your behind. But as Mark Twain said about Wagner's music: "It's not as bad as it sounds."

We can all grow. We can hone our skills and talents. We can learn to climb mountains we never thought possible. This knowledge drives me on.

When I first took on an assignment for Wadley Cancer Center in Dallas, the staff took me through its research department. I was much impressed. I saw men and women in their white gowns, test tubes whirling in some mysterious centrifugal fashion, and tissues being examined in vacuum-type contraptions. Everyone seemed very serious and intense. I spoke in whispers. I didn't understand any of it, but I was greatly affected.

After the tour of the laboratories, the staff took me to a small room where I was shown a film done in time-sequence. It was amazing. Breathtaking. The film covered a period of six months, but in 90 seconds, I saw a healthy cell attacked by a cancer cell. I saw the healthy cell succumb, and finally become totally absorbed by the cancer. Then they showed me, in time-sequence, a healthy cell injected with interferon. Interferon is manufactured at Wadley, one of only two places in the country where it is produced. In 90 seconds, I saw the healthy cell attacked by cancer. It was repelled. It attacked again. Repelled! Attacked again. Repelled again! Finally, the cancer dissipated. It was gone. It was a powerful demonstration. It was a miracle, and I had seen it all on film. I tell you, I was moved. I was overwhelmed. I was also darned proud to be associated with an institution that was so dramatically involved in saving lives.

When we walked out of the viewing, Dudley Rouse, who heads the program at Wadley, put his hand on my arm. We stopped for a moment. "Jerry, if you help us raise the money we need, you will be as important in conquering cancer as any of our scientists."

Me! I could conquer cancer. Me, the fundraiser—I could really save lives. Well! I flew as an eagle. I was at the peak of the mountain, and I could have gone even higher. I was ecstatic.

And during the time I worked with Wadley, we led the race. We beat Sloane-Kettering into the first trial in an important new discovery. And we beat M.D. Anderson. And Genentech. And a Japanese firm. And we beat them all into second trials.

Thank you, Lord. I was helping to conquer cancer. It was glorious!

If you found at times my light tone turning into a sermon, just keep in mind that this is the inspirational reading. The hell and damnation part!

I went into the writing with considerable trepidation. I was one with Stendahl: "Who am I? What have I done? What do I know? If I write it all down, I may find out."

I discovered in the research and the writing that we must take advantage of every opportunity. I guess I knew this, but now it was confirmed. Strike while the iron is hot. Strike when it is even merely warm! A career passes so quickly.

Someone once told me that my career has had five stages: (1) Who is Jerry Panas? (2) Get me Jerry Panas. (3) We need someone like Jerry Panas. (4) What we need is a young Jerry Panas. (5) Who is Jerry Panas? I believe that I am somewhere between stages two and three. My friends indicate that I am somewhere in stage four, moving quickly into stage five! I take considerable consolation in what I heard a speaker say at a conference recently: "I used to be an eccentric. Now I am an expert. I was once told, now I am consulted. I have graduated from being somebody who should know better to somebody who knows better. The only wisdom I now claim is that I have continued doing for many years what I have always been doing. And it seems to work."

As for me, as a result of this research, I am even more determined to persevere and strive to grow. I'll be stronger in will, determined to survive, to seek, to find, and not to yield. I'll work harder than I ever have. I won't give in, I won't give up. I shall be the best I can possibly be.

I was particularly moved by something that happened to me recently. I won't use the right names. That would be too close to home. But other than the names, everything else is exactly as it happened.

I was asked to make a call with the president of a college on the chairman of his board. It was a natural. The college was involved in a $70 million campaign and the president and the chairman were close friends. And the chairman was very wealthy. In a sense, I was going along for the ride, to be used as an outside voice. But the president didn't need any help. He did it all.

The president—I'll call him Simon—and I went into the chairman's office. Let's call the chairman Tom.

I wish you could have been there with me. It was magnificent. The best lesson I've ever had in fundraising. A graduate degree. Here's what happened.

We spent a few minutes just chattering and then Simon started. "Tom, tell Jerry how you happened to come to our college as a student. It's a great story."

"Well, it's really the most important thing that happened in my life. I was the last of four children and none of my brothers or sisters were able to go to college. We just didn't have enough money. But my high school counselor told me about this small college that had a scholarship given by an anonymous donor. He thought I might qualify. I visited the campus and fell totally in love with it. And you wouldn't believe it—I not only got the scholarship, but they let me wait on tables, wash the dishes, and do the landscaping around the campus. I was able to get all of my tuition free and work for my room and board. It was wonderful."

And then, Simon again: "That's a great story, but tell Jerry how you happened to meet Susie. That's really very special."

"Well one day, I was raking the leaves and I looked across the quadrangle and I saw this girl and I thought, Lord, she's beautiful. I'm going to marry that girl. I threw down my rake, ran across the quadrangle, and introduced myself. I chased her for two years and she finally agreed to marry me. We were married in the college chapel."

Simon then talked to Tom about his gift to the campaign. It was a very persuasive request but the truth is, Tom really sold himself. Simon merely provided the opportunity. He's a master at it. Tom made a gift of $6 million to the campaign.

I've thought a great deal about that meeting and what happened. I ask you, who is the real hero of that story?

The hero is Tom. Wrong! Tom had the money to make the gift. More than that, everything he had in life, he owed to the college. He's not the hero.

The hero is President Simon. He got the gift. Wrong again! Simon was in the best position possible to get the gift. He was a friend of the chairman, probably his best friend. And anyway, the chief executive officer of an institution or a staff person is most often the best person to get the gift.

The hero of the story is the anonymous donor who provided the scholarship. Well, still not quite right. You're wrong again.

The real hero of the story is the fundraiser who was on that campus at the time who persuaded the anonymous donor to make the gift. That scholarship made possible the $6 million gift to the campaign—and the fundraiser did it. He or she, whoever it was, is the hero.

I've thought a lot about Tom's gift. And the anonymous donor. And the hero—the fundraiser. How wonderful to be in a profession where we all have the opportunity to be a hero. How glorious to be part of a bold adventure. A sense of mission. The ministry of opportunity. Working at great causes and with magnificent people.

I have stopped often in the writing of my manuscript to ask for the strength and inspiration to make the words a proper tribute to fundraising and a celebration of the wonderful men and women who give their devotion and commitment to changing and saving lives. You are all heroes, and in heaven you will surely stand on the right hand of the martyrs.

This book is dedicated to all who toil in the great exploration of fundraising, with deep affection and appreciation most especially for the professionals and volunteers with whom I have served. Together, we have worked and dreamed. We have known despair and have won noble victories. We have labored sedulously and joyfully at changing and saving lives. We have given witness that there is something greater, something outside ourselves that makes us all heroes. How lucky we are.

To all the fundraisers and volunteers I have worked with, I owe you an immense debt. You have given me much more than I can ever repay. In his *East of Eden*, John Steinbeck wrote: "You came upon me carving some kind of little figure out of wood and you said, 'why don't you make something for me?' I asked you what you wanted, and you said, 'a box.'"

"What for?"

"To put things in."

"What things?"

"Whatever you have," you said.

"Well, here's your box. Nearly everything I have is in it, and it is not full. Pain and excitement are in it, and feeling good or bad, and evil thoughts and good thoughts—the pleasure of design and some despair and an indescribable joy of creation.

"And on top of these are all the gratitude and love I have for you.

"And still the box is not full."

16   One Final Note

About midway through the writing of this book, it occurred to me that I didn't know how to handle the word. Come on now, you know what I'm talking about—THE word.

Is it one word, two words, or hyphenated?

There's an infallible rule that governs precisely this situation. If it's an adjective, it's one word: fundraising. If it's a noun, two words: fund raising. Or is it the other way around? In any case, I am certain that the rule is inviolate.

I called some people I consider authorities in our field. I spoke to Ursula Ellis, one of the senior officers at NAHD. She told me that she wasn't really sure how it was handled at headquarters. "We have no real policy around here about that and I guess each staff person handles the word as he or she chooses. I think I usually use two words for both the noun and the adjective. And I'm not sure about the verb—I guess two words, also."

I called Dick Wilson, executive director of the NSFRE. He always knows about this sort of thing.

"Dick, I have this serious problem. When you use it, is it fundraising, fund raising, or fund-raising?"

There was a long pause. "I make it two words all the time. But hold on a minute, we have a glossary around here somewhere that we printed a couple years ago that governs that sort of thing. We felt that we needed a rule so that everyone would know the proper thing to do. There's been a lot of confusion about this. Let me see if I can find a glossary."

The phone was silent for a long time. Dick finally returned. "Well I'll be darned. In the glossary, we say that the word should be hyphenated all the time—for a noun, adjective, or verb. I guess I've been doing it wrong all this time."

"Well, do you think you'll change?"

"I guess I'll keep doing it the way I have."

I rather agree with Dick's sentiment regarding the matter. Glossary or not, seeing the word hyphenated just somehow doesn't look right to me.

I knew what to do. I called John J. Schwartz. For years, Jack was president of the AAFRC, and one of the nation's leading spokesmen on fundraising. (Or fund-raising, if you have a bias for the glossary.) If anyone would know, Jack would. I've never known him to equivocate on anything. And actually, never to be in doubt on anything. "Jack, I have this problem." And I explained my dilemma.

There was this long pause. Somehow in this investigation, I've learned a lot about long pauses!

"To tell the truth, I don't know if there is a rule about this sort of thing and I don't believe anybody is really consistent about it."

"How do you handle the word, John?"

"Well, I use two words. But that's just by preference. Let me see if I've got any material around here." Long pause. "Well, this is interesting. Here's a piece from AAFRC where it's hyphenated, and here's an article in a magazine where it is two words, and here's a folder where they use it both ways." We spoke some more and finally decided that I probably ought to make it two words. That seemed to make the most sense.

About 20 minutes later I had a telephone call. It was Jack Schwartz. He said that he had just checked with the office at AAFRC and there's definitely a rule and a style. The word—whether it's a noun, an adjective, or a verb—is to be hyphenated.

Good grief. I just don't like that hyphen.

So I called my publisher and reported the puzzle and the results of my investigation. He somehow didn't show the same kind of passion for the matter that I did. I said: "Aaron, it seems to me that no one really knows, and I definitely don't like the hyphen. Let's decide what to do. The important thing is that we be consistent.

"Let's make the noun and the adjective one word. I really like it that way and it looks good to me. And let's hyphenate the verb."

It really didn't matter a lot to me, hyphenating the verb. I don't use it very much—in fact, I don't think I used it as a verb once in my manuscript. And I didn't even know it was supposed to have a hyphen.

So I said to Aaron: "The important thing is to be consistent. Nouns and adjectives, one word. Verbs are hyphenated."

I believe it was Sally Rand, the famous Fan Dancer, who was asked to explain her immense success. "I owe it all to the two most important rules of advertising: Always be consistent and follow the principle of using plenty of white space."

Appendix I
The Most Important Criteria

On this page are 88 criteria—skills, talents, characteristics, and attributes—which comprised the original list that is described in this book. An additional item, Impeccable Integrity, was added later. This made a total of 89 criteria.

After a careful selection process, the original list was reduced to 30 criteria, and on this page they are noted with an asterisk (*). This smaller group of factors became the basis for the questionnaires which were distributed and used for the in-depth interviewing of 48 men and women who were part of the critical sampling.

Be creative*
Have perseverance*
Have presence*
Enjoy pressure
Have high self-esteem
Be a long-range planner
Be a people-person*
Have personal style
Be a careful planner*
Be a conceptualizer*
Have a concern for society
Love the work*
Have a religious motivation
Be a good writer
Have a concern for people*
Be planning oriented
Be intense
Be spontaneous
Have a happy home life
Be a perfectionist
Be impulsive
Be self-sufficient
Be independent
Have spiritual motivation
Be decisive
Be a workaholic
Be assertive
Be a good speaker
Be physically attractive
Be a strong supervisor
Emphasize attention to detail
Be a good listener*
Be flexible

Be a strong strategist*
Be socially inclined
Be highly intelligent
Be persuasive*
Be active in professional society
Have ability to deal with rejection
Be a survivor
Have a quality of leadership*
Be well educated
Be convincing*
Have strong communication skills*
Have impeccable integrity (added later)*
Enjoy long-term relationships
Be hard working*
Need recognition
Seek challenges
Be a self-starter*
Be a risk taker
Be action oriented*
Have high expectations*
Be hungry to win
Be able to see the big picture*
Have a social concern
Have a committed belief in the organization
Be self-disciplined*
Have high physical energy

Like people*
Be articulate*
Handle stress well
Have excellent health
Handle pressure well
Have high visibility
Have high energy*
Be an extrovert
Have ability to motivate people*
Be goal oriented*
Know campaign mechanics
Have class
Be resilient
Be aggressive
Be rigid
Be persistent
Have a sense of humor
Have above average intelligence
Be eager to succeed
Have good working relationship with other staff
Be consistent
Have ingenuity
Have ability to inspire action*
Be an effective salesman*
Have a business sense
Be bright*
Be empathetic
Be well organized*

* used for the final sampling

Appendix II
Appraisal of Success Factors

The Appraisal of Success Factors is a listing of the 20 skills, attributes, and characteristics which are deemed to be the most significant in fundraising. They are weighted to reflect their importance. Take for instance your evaluation of Factor #2—"Good Listener." Let's say that you give yourself a "9" for this factor. The Weighted Value is four. Multiply your evaluation times four: 9x4=36. Give yourself a "9" in Column A and a "36" in Column C.

There are four columns:

A. The Self-Appraisal. Your evaluation of your own qualities for each factor.

C. Your Weighted Evaluation. Multiply Column A times Column B.

B. The Weighted Value. Multiply this number times your evaluation in Column A.

D. Maximum Number of Points Possible. The highest evaluation—a "ten," times the weighted value.

In Column A, score "1" to "10" for each item—1 being the lowest, 10 the highest. An evaluation of 4 or below would indicate an unacceptable appraisal or one which requires a great deal of improvement; 5 or 6, an appraisal at an acceptable level, but not of special merit; 7 or 8, a superior standard; 9, exceptional level; 10, the highest possible score, a peak performance.

Four extra spaces (#21 through #24) are allotted for any criteria you, your supervisor, board, or committee wish to add which are felt to be peculiarly significant to you and your institution.

THE FACTORS	WEIGHTED VALUE	A	B	C	D
1. Impeccable Integrity	5 times Evaluation		X 5		50
2. Good Listener	4 times Evaluation		X 4		40
3. Ability to Motivate	3 times Evaluation		X 3		30
4. Hard Worker	3 times Evaluation		X 3		30
5. Concern for People	3 times Evaluation		X 3		30
6. High Expectations	3 times Evaluation		X 3		30
7. Love The Work	3 times Evaluation		X 3		30
8. High Energy	3 times Evaluation		X 3		30
9. Perseverance	3 times Evaluation		X 3		30
10. Presence	3 times Evaluation		X 3		30
11. Self-Confidence	3 times Evaluation		X 3		30
12. Common Sense	2 times Evaluation		X 2		20
13. Strong Communication Skill	2 times Evaluation		X 2		20
14. Quality of Leadership	2 times Evaluation		X 2		20
15. Creative	2 times Evaluation		X 2		20
16. Ability to Inspire Action	2 times Evaluation		X 2		20
17. Self-Starter	1 times Evaluation		X 1		10
18. Well Organized	1 times Evaluation		X 1		10
19. Strong Strategist	1 times Evaluation		X 1		10
20. Goal Oriented	1 times Evaluation		X 1		10
21.					
22.					
23.					
24.					
	TOTAL				500

INDEX (for the first twenty factors only)

450-500	A peak performer—one of the great!
400-449	Exceptional
350-399	Superior
300-349	Good
299 & Below	Needs work!

SPECIAL NOTE

(1) For a proper assessment, in addition to your own self-appraisal, you should have your supervisor and key volunteer leaders complete the ASF also.

(2) It may surprise you that "experience" or "productivity" is not listed a significant factor. The basis of this is that in actuality, they are not major criteria in determining your success. Experience is not important. And if you score well on the ASF, your productivity will automatically be high.

(3) For your particular situation, if you chose to add "productivity," you may use #21.

(4) If you do add any factors beyond the 20 listed, you will have to allow for this and adjust the INDEX.